THOMISM IN AN AGE OF RENEWAL

RALPH M. McINERNY

THOMISM
IN AN AGE OF RENEWAL

1966

DOUBLEDAY & COMPANY, INC.

GARDEN CITY, NEW YORK

Nihil obstat: Edward J. Montano, S.T.D.
     Censor librorum
Imprimatur: ✠ Terence J. Cooke, D.D., V.G.
     Archdiocese of New York
     August 11, 1966

The nihil obstat and imprimatur are official declarations that a book or pamphlet is free of doctrinal or moral error. No implication is contained therein that those who have granted the nihil obstat and imprimatur agree with the contents, opinions, or statements expressed.

In Memoriam
Charles DeKoninck

PREFACE

Books, like children, inspire a split of spirit in their authors. On the one hand, we feel they ought, when they go out into the world, to speak for themselves; on the other hand, there is an impulse to explain them, even to apologize for them. In the case of children, pointing to their lineage to excuse their faults is fair enough, but with books that sort of thing is less seemly. To develop the comparison to the point of a conceit, in the literary sense, I notice how enthralled my children are with the story of how I met their mother. Perhaps what grips them, as they try to peer into that unsettling past, prior to any present of theirs, is the thought of how easily they might not have been. Books cannot be expected to quiver with a consciousness of the contingency of things, of course, but perhaps the reader will be interested in a brief account of how this book came to be written. It is certainly no product of planned parenthood.

During the spring semester of 1965, Father Cornelio Fabro was Visiting Professor at the University of Notre Dame. I had been reading him for years; while doing my doctoral dissertation I had made use of his Italian edition of Kierkegaard's *Journals*, which contains many scholarly and illuminating notes; during my first year of teaching I read his *La nozione metafisica di partecipazione*. Subsequently, I read much of what he has written. His scope, his scholarship, his boundless interests caused me to think of him as a member of that small group of truly top-flight Thomists. It was a pleasure, therefore, to have him at my own university and to find that he is every bit as interesting a person as he is a scholar. In March of 1965 an article of Father Fabro's, entitled *Tomismo di Domani,* "The Thomism of Tomorrow," appeared in *L'Osservatore Romano.* My colleague Professor Joseph Bobik and I were much taken with the article and undertook to put it into English. Unfortunately, the article found no home in an American publication; we really have no counterpart to the continental weekly newspaper. Father Thurston Davis, the editor of *America,* found Father Fabro's article simply too long for his publication but asked me if I would care to do something along the same lines. The result was an article bearing the same title as this book's, which appeared in September 1965. I received a great many letters in the weeks following its publication from Catholic thinkers of widely different interests and persuasions, and the majority professed to find in what I had written something with which to agree. Thus encouraged, I was in a receptive mood when I was contacted by Mr. J. F. Bernard of Doubleday, who wanted to know if I would be interested in developing my thoughts at book length. Apparently I was.

Thanks to Pope John XXIII, we live in an age of renewal in the Church. The Council, which is his true legacy, has been concluded, but its work will continue in other forms. To renew involves, of course, a disturbance of much that has become familiar, a putting away in favor of an essential conservation. There are many who fancy themselves at opposite extremes who have yet reacted in a basically similar fashion to what has been going on because they have both tended, I think, to confuse the accidental with the essential. There have been some who gave the impression, almost, that if the liturgy can be changed, so too can the Ten Commandments; there have been others who seemed to feel that, since the liturgy has been changed, nothing is the same. Both extremes have done a lot of lamenting during the past several years: the Fathers of the Council were dragging their feet and impeding progress. Or, the Fathers of the Council had lost their wits and were doing imprudent and dangerous things. Those who are called liberals sometimes acted as if the Council were a private possession of theirs which, by some subtle strategy, they had foisted on a resisting Church and which, in the event, was wrested from their hands by the bishops, of all people, and turned to whatever degree from its intended direction. Those who are called conservatives seemed to concede much of that claim but to feel the liberal impulse had not been sufficiently checked. Surely by now we must realize that the Council belongs to the Church, that is, to all of us. It represents neither a partisan victory nor a partisan defeat but the *ecclesia docens*. Its decrees are neither liberal nor conservative, mine nor yours, but ours, and our response to their letter and spirit should be wholehearted and complete.

In the present essay I have attempted to discuss the status of Thomism in the present situation. There were those who awaited its dethronement by the Council; there were others who expected a stiffer restatement of earlier directives. Both, I suppose, have been disappointed. It would be difficult to work up sympathy either for those who hoped Aquinas would be supplanted by existentialism or phenomenology or Teilhard de Chardin; it would be equally difficult to sympathize with those who felt that all was as it should be with Catholic philosophy. As it happens, the Council had very little to say on the matter of philosophy, and this may seem to leave the matter quite ambiguous. What is the status of all those ecclesiastical documents concerning the philosophy of St. Thomas, those going back to Leo XIII, but those as well that go back many centuries before Leo? Are we to suppose, in the absence of any detailed discussion of them, that they have been superseded? And, if so, by what? Has Thomas Aquinas fallen from favor? Is Thomism in or out? These are some of the questions to which I try to address myself in the discussion which follows. What I have to say does not pretend to be the last word on questions so important; neither does this essay contain my first thoughts on the matter discussed. Like most Catholic philosophers, I have been reflecting on the question of Thomism almost from the beginning of my studies. It is my earnest hope that nothing I say here will do disservice to the thought of Aquinas. If, in some small way, I can convince the well disposed but wary that their philosophizing has everything to gain and nothing to lose by going to Thomas, I will be more than content.

I will not bore the reader or embarrass my friends by mentioning all those who, over the years, have helped me to achieve what little clarity I have on the topics I discuss here. This book is dedicated, as a modest token of gratitude, to the memory of an inspiring teacher and a dear friend. May he rest in peace.

February 1966
Notre Dame, Indiana

CONTENTS

THOMISM IN AN AGE OF RENEWAL

CHAPTER ONE
INTRODUCTORY

The word "philosophize" means both "to inquire whether we ought to philosophize or not" and "to devote oneself to philosophical speculation." Aristotle, Protrepticus

The story about Thales and the well is too good to be true, so it has become symbolic. Any aspiration to wisdom, any attempt to go beyond the common sense of the plain man to attain a sapiential over-view, runs the risk of reducing us to a condition inferior to that of the practical man of affairs. More often than not, the philosopher steps for the elevator only to get the shaft and in those nether regions to which he then plummets he may find himself less concerned to resume philosophizing than to consider just what it was he was doing before he fell. But that, as Aristotle observed, is yet another instance of philosophizing. It was once thought to be characteristic of man that he not only acts but reflects on his activity. There is much to be said for the view. It is surely the case that, from the dawn of philosophy, one of its recurrent problems has been the nature of philosophy itself. In the essay which follows, we shall be engaged in philosophizing of a second order, philosophizing about philosophy and about philosophizing, not in all the generality that suggests, of course, but with reference to the recent resurgence of discontent with Thomism. The discontent to which I refer has sought to take its warrant from Pope John's call for *aggiornamento*, for an updating and renewal within the Church. And since Thomism, for better or worse, has long been bound up with the Church's intellectual apostolate, both philosophical and theological, it is hardly surprising that Pope John's call for renewal has been taken as an invitation to reflect critically on Thomism. This critical reflection has been both good and bad—more bad than good, I think, and I am referring to the quality of the discussion. It is into this murky area that I propose to enter now.

Something of the disillusion of the unrequited is often evident in remarks about Thomism. With a shock that is profound but certainly not speechless, it dawns upon the incipient critic that most philosophers who lay claim to the title of Thomist are pretty miserable thinkers, not exactly electric in the classroom and painfully narrow in their interests and information. The day this realization comes can be a dark one and in its want of light a sometimes mordant, often humorous, frequently telling rhetoric is born. Categories take shape, a typology is devised. One becomes aware of Thomists of the strict observance; of calced and discalced Thomists; of Thomists who proceed as do, in another field, New Critics; of Thomists who approach the text as the focal point of a network of historical relations. There emerge to the wondering eye existential Thomists and—though this is rather by accusation than claim—essentialistic Thomists; there are phenomenological Thomists and analytical Thomists. And, in a classic of *Timese*, there are even Peeping Thomists. Psychologists make a characteristic contribution and, if they don't exactly reduce Thomism to breast feeding, locate the phenomenon at a certain stage of childish intelligence.

In this twilight of the student soul, a vast distaste begins. How can any, let alone all, of this be relevant? (Relevance becomes an absolute in the rhetoric to which we refer.) If one would speak to his contemporaries, he must take on their coloration. If Thomism is irrelevant, let us then turn to contemporary philosophy. Now this exhortation, so seemingly simple, so often made, is far more difficult to heed than is commonly recognized, for to what contemporary philosophy are we to turn? There is no such thing as contemporary philosophy, of course, at least if this is construed as some sum total of commonly held tenets of the day. There are contemporary philosophies, philosophies as numerous, one sometimes thinks, as philosophers. And it is at once an impressive and depressing thought that there may be more professional philosophers alive at this moment than have graced the planet in all previous ages together, this in a time when philosophy is under siege, both from within and without, when its territory, because of the erosion and occupation which have been going on for centuries, is next to non-existent. There seems so little left for the philosopher specifically to do; whole regions and continents of his domain have "come of age" and metamorphosed into sciences. One entire wing of contemporary philosophy may be seen as simply acquiescing to this rape and contenting itself with a tireless and all too often tedious parsing of the sentences scientists emit—when they speak a parsable language—while another wing seeks to re-occupy territory ceded long since to the poet. The wings of which I speak are hardly usable categories, of course. The historian of philosophy has trouble enough with past ages, but his problems become impossible when he tries to follow the moving finger of his own day. How then those blithe spirits who speak of the imperative need to recast in "existential" terms the message of the Church? If their motive is to ingratiate themselves with some putative *zeitgeist*, they are culpably unaware of the uncounted tribes of certified philosophers who would be left icy cold by such prestidigitation. The difficulties "scholastic terminology" is alleged to present to the "modern mind" are as nothing to the difficulties many modern minds encounter when they attempt to read an existentialist (who, if he is worth his salt, will decline the epithet). A phenomenological approach—most often undefined—is a variant of the existential prescription for relevance, but the most thorough and authoritative history of the phenomenological movement does not succeed, in two volumes, in discerning what precisely phenomenology or the phenomenological method is. Indeed, when as if in despair its learned author seeks to sum up his most informative work by performing a phenomenological analysis, this reader has the distinct and disappointed feeling that he might be reading a chapter of Book Delta of the *Metaphysics,* or Augustine, or Alcuin, or Abelard, or. . . . But why go on? The much touted revolutionary method is fuller of echoes than of new notes.

Now, as I hope will emerge from the sequel, the author of the present essay is not uninterested in contemporary philosophies. Indeed, I shall argue that the very spirit of Thomism requires an endless openness to whatever philosophizing goes on; Thomism, in short, is not a closed system. But more of that anon. My present target is that fuzzy mind which, understandably and often justifiably put off by the Thomism of many texts and classrooms, bids goodbye to all that and turns with relief and uncritical admiration to a monolith which, being non-existent, can only be mythical, namely, "contemporary philosophy." It is a holy and wholesome thought to go beyond Thomism, in the sense of what St. Thomas himself knew and wrote, but it is surely axiomatic that one cannot go beyond before he has caught up. A distaste for Thomism, however understandably acquired, is not a critique of Thomism. Simply to ignore St. Thomas should be recognized for what it is, ignorance of St. Thomas, and not billed as a thought-out replacement for the role the Common Doctor of the Church has been chosen to play. For every specific and textual criticism of St. Thomas there seem to be a hundred tirades launched out of a pique so mindless one would like only to be amused were such tirades not bruited about as intelligent instances of *aggiornamento*. These counterfeits of argument lead to the issuance of promissory notes bearing the watermark of relevance which function as good money so long as it is not noticed that their sources are, if possible, more innocent of "contemporary philosophy" than they are of the doctrines they so cheerfully claim to go beyond.

Needless to say, the foregoing paragraphs do not refer to those many thinkers who, whether because of or despite the literary forms assumed by responses to the Church's recommendation of St. Thomas, have absorbed the doctrine of their master and then gone beyond it in many directions. Gilson, Maritain, DeKoninck, Fabro, Pieper, Rahner, Dondeyne, Lonergan—one feels the list should not even be begun because, no matter how lengthy, it would be incomplete. I fear that I shall never forget the young priest who, in the common room of a major seminary where I was visiting, launched without preliminary into an attack on a Maritain he had not read on a point he could not possibly have given previous thought to with a vehemence that crescendoed as his coherence decrescendoed. With a wave of his pink perspiring hand he disdainfully dismissed a lifetime of intellectual effort by a man from whom anyone can learn. In that encounter I came to suspect that humor is the only adequate defense against these latter-day Cornificians and I wish to confer on that young man the status of a paradigm for purposes of this essay. Certainly the stature of Maritain, being utterly unmeasured by that strident critic, could scarcely have been trimmed by what he said. But the simple fact is that such outbursts have become commonplace; they cannot be ignored; they should be displayed for the mirth they unwittingly evoke. What is pardonable, at least as a passing phase, in an undergraduate is reprehensible in those who may seem to the uninstructed to be speaking with something resembling authority. For it is a melancholy truth that the horizon is cluttered with the hasty triptychs of iconoclasts; that few are less flexible than they who assail dogma; that the dullest monologists hold forth on the necessity of dialogue; that a little philosophy is a dangerous thing.

The level on which I begin, then, is one on which I hope to address myself to my paradigmatic young man. A superficial level, therefore; the level of the bull session, that inevitable refuge in the springtime of our discontent. I am not being condescending. This is the level on which most of us usually are and it is there that attacks are made on Thomism, on seminary education, on the curricula of our Catholic colleges. My point thus far has to do with the maladroitness of archers rather than the absence of a target. Thomism is open to criticism and it is open to defense, but only on the assumption that we know what it is that we are criticizing and what it is that we are defending. This is not merely a matter of definition, of course; it must be insisted upon that one can enter the discussion only if he is qualified to do so—provided he wants to be taken seriously. Curiously enough, those who say most emphatically that they learned no philosophy in college or seminary seem to assume that that all too obvious fact equips them as critics of philosophy and philosophical curricula. But no doubt they have become Renaissance men in the interval. In an age of auto-suggestion and self-appointment, the reminder must be made that we are dealing with serious matters when we speak of the philosophy of Christians, that in this area more is required than the drive for

self-expression. What is at issue cannot be decided by a pleb-
iscite with each man having one vote whatever his credentials.
In an atmosphere where adolescents in minor seminaries are
urged to turn their uncluttered minds on the question of
clerical celibacy, its pros and cons and doubtful future, one
may seem the enemy of democratic ideals if he reacts by saying he has not the faintest interest in the results of such
fledgling efforts, adding that he is shocked by the suggestion that discussion profits in direct ratio to the incompe-
tence of the interlocutors. One notices that the same priests
who apologize for what they regard as clerical and in-
competent statements on marriage themselves sail onward
into discussions of conjugal intimacies which are at once em-
barrassingly graphic and hilariously wonderlandish.

But let us return to an earlier, perhaps concealed, admission. Most Thomists, we said, are pretty miserable thinkers, not exactly electric in the classroom and painfully narrow in their interests and information. Say that is true. I
think it is; I am a Thomist, or try to be, and I have no illusion
about being unequivocally included in the "some" my "most"
requires for contrast. All right. For whatever comfort it
provides, we could equally well and truly say that most
philosophers are pretty miserable thinkers, not exactly electric in the classroom and painfully narrow in their interests
and information. Furthermore, it could be truly claimed that
Thomists have a penchant for dismissing, under the guise of
refuting, positions they do not comprehend, for pigeonhol-
ing real or imaginary adversaries, for racking up cheap vic-
tories over absent and unmet rivals before classrooms of perhaps impressed students. But as much can be said of most
philosophers without qualification of school and persuasion.
Now I am not impressed with the force of this *tu quoque*;
the "So's your old man" argument may make sibling rivals

out of just plain rivals but it doesn't redeem dear old Dad. What I want to get out of this unsettling parallel is simply this. The real or considered failure of one's philosophical seniors is not as such an argument against philosophy; indeed, seriously to make this appraisal requires that one perform, and perform well, the activity he judges to be performed badly by those he criticizes. This is the paradox of anti-philosophy, insisted on from the beginning. By the same token, if one feels that he can seriously and without rancor or *superbia vitae* make the judgment about Thomists stated above, the conclusion to be drawn, I should think, is not that we must bid a fond or unfond adieu to Thomas Aquinas. One would be better advised to ask what, in the species of Thomism one reacts against, has gone wrong, wherein has it failed, what ameliorations in the response to the Church's invitation that we take Thomas as our guide are possible and desirable. In a word, it seems to me, that for the Catholic the only valid criticism of the Thomism that is the going concern of a given day is the initiation of a more adequate, less flawed, more defensible Thomism. That is a claim that requires more than my hearty assurance, to be sure, and I shall be trying later to show that alternatives to this suggestion are not true options for the Catholic.

It used to be said, some years back, and this was a serious suggestion which I don't wish to lampoon, that the ecclesiastical directives having to do with the role of St. Thomas referred to seminaries and not to Catholic colleges whose clientele are laymen. The reason for the directives, the suggestion continued, lay in the fact that seminarians had to learn the language of the Scholastic theology they would later study. Even in those days, when I felt a good deal less irenic on this question than I have subsequently become, it struck me as an odd notion that what by implication was treated as an inferior philosophy might be good enough for future priests but would hardly do for the laity. (This was long before the current ascendancy of the layman.) The judgment that Scholastic philosophy is at best a vocabulary for theology at least exhibited a laudable sensitivity to the need for a precise language with which to confess our faith and reason about its contents. But, as even the proponents of this suggestion would doubtless have agreed, this is a poor defense of the traditional Catholic philosophy. I mention it now for several reasons. First, I do not regard this as the Church's real reason for preferring the philosophy of St. Thomas. Second, it serves as a preparation for our later discussion of the paradox of Thomistic terminology. Why is it that courses in Thomism have sometimes seemed very much like courses in a foreign language, a kind of churchy Esperanto to be learned like any jargon? That this should have come about is a profound betrayal of St. Thomas; its remedy can be found by having recourse to what I at least take to be the true philosophical significance of some current inquiries which are called phenomenological.

Another kind of discussion that went on in more halcyon days, when it was not considered gauche to admit that the Church had indeed expressed Herself on the role of St. Thomas, had to do with the degree of the individual Catholic's obligation to abide by the Church's wish. It is only a suggestion, it used to be said, we don't *have* to do things that way. I was reluctant then, and I am equally reluctant now, to discuss the presence, let alone the degree, of guilt in this attitude. Perhaps some will find it indicative of galloping docility on my part, but I did find this a strange reaction and, in my simplicity, likened it to a child's acting contrary to the wishes of its parents simply because the wish had not been stated in the form of a command. Whence the delight in saying the advice was not binding and obligatory when it emanated from a source whose only concern is our welfare? And, in the case of philosophy, what else could the Church wish to have fare well than our reason? Isn't it obvious that, if the Church suggests we begin the study of philosophy with St. Thomas, the first and obvious basis for this advice would be the judgment that to follow it would be to achieve the desired term of philosophizing? Normally when parents suggest one route among many to their children, it is because that route leads more surely to the goal. To take delight in the fact that one is not prevented, under penalty, from taking the long way round or a *cul-de-sac* is an elation I find it difficult to share.

It is not unlikely that what others in their turn found difficult to bear in the contrary attitude was a kind of smugness among Thomists, their suggestion that nothing awaited them over any horizon you could name but a sensation of *déjà vu:* horizons need a sun and surely there is nothing new beneath that. For Thomism can become a shield and an excuse: a shield against disturbing novelties and an excuse for intellectual lethargy. The *opera omnia* of Aquinas—and here and there a few Thomists contacted Thomistic texts elsewhere than in citations in manuals—were treated as if they were an encyclopedia. Somewhere in the more manipulable Parma, if not in the sandwich-board size volumes of the incomplete Leonine edition, was the answer to any question you could succeed in framing; like a lawyer preparing a brief, the dutiful Thomist was assured of his precedents; he had only to marshal the material to fit the special difficulty. When one wasn't struck by their diversity, one was assailed by the thought that Thomists constituted a kind of international Mafia or Cosa Nostra; the invitation to philosophize which, in the beginning, its attraction undiminished by our vague conception of what it was, seemed a call to a solitary and lonely enterprise suddenly became more like an enrollment in a fraternal elite. One half expected to be taught the special handclasp. I had the good fortune to do some of my graduate work at Laval University, where I studied under Charles DeKoninck. Once at a convention, after I had been teaching for a few years, a nun I had never met before, discovering my past, broke into the most conspiratorial smile and whispered, "Ah, you're one of Charlie's boys!" The little wave she gave me when she left was not the secret sign, only a merry benediction, but it was clear I had been rescued from limbo at least in virtue of a shared teacher. On the wider scene, Aquinas too is sometimes treated as if he were the shared talisman of the initiate. Small wonder that it all appears less than enticing to many. There are not a few anthologies containing sections entitled "Marxism and Thomism." When Thomism becomes a party line, it is not surprising that many prefer a private number.

In case it should need overt mention, I wish to make it clear that, with respect to Thomism, I stand no nearer the obscurantist devotees than I do the kookie critics of it. For that is simply not the option and it never was. What I shall be arguing for in what follows is not the "official view"; I am not sure what it is, or indeed if there is one, in the areas we shall explore. Thomism has become institutionalized, there is no doubt about that, and it is a matter we shall discuss. But what I shall be doing is expressing one man's response to the clear invitation of the Church that he begin the study of philosophy with St. Thomas Aquinas. That is the side of the matter I shall stress. The invitation is addressed to you and the question is, what will your response be? There is no sense thinking the matter can be dissolved by a sociological analysis of Thomism as an institution. *You* can't let the mat-

ter go by arch observations on how *they* reacted to it. If I
wanted to be timely, I could say I am going to stress the
existential side of the question. I speak without authority, save
that of my arguments and interpretations; I am not attempting to wrap myself in the mantle of orthodoxy, a corner of
which I offer you for salvific cover. But I do hope to dissipate
some of the nonsense that has spread over the land. Paint as
black a picture as you like of the current situation of Thomism and I feel confident a few more daubs could be added.
But remember that the same thing could be done with philosophy, period. The question remains, what next?

In recent years a distinction has been drawn between the
teaching of St. Thomas and the Thomistic tradition. Gilson
and Fabro, with somewhat different emphases, have insisted
on the distinction, both feeling that over the centuries what
St. Thomas taught tended to become obscured and distorted
in the writings of his followers. This may not seem to be a
serious matter, but the fact is that some followers of Thomas
greet the eye within the Leonine edition of Aquinas' two
summae. Cajetan's commentary on the *Summa theologiae*
and Sylvester of Ferrara's commentary on the *Summa contra
gentes* are printed along with the texts they comment. Furthermore, both the *Cursus philosophicus* and the *Cursus
theologicus* of John of St. Thomas have taken on a privileged status as authoritative expositions of the thought of the
Angelic Doctor. It is easy to appreciate the dismay felt by
one who thinks these commentators have distorted the
thought of Aquinas to find their writings almost as accessible
and prominent as those of St. Thomas himself. He would prefer to separate Thomas from the Thomistic tradition, to res-
cue Aquinas from his followers. Now there can be no question of our entering into this criticism here, but there is a
variation on the suggested separation that we can argue for.

If it is true that the favor the Church has shown Aquinas does not transfer automatically to his friends and commentators, it is equally true that we need not equate the role Aquinas is meant to play in our intellectual life with past or present curricular interpretations and implementations of that role. Someday, no doubt, an intrepid historian will be found who will undertake to describe what has happened to St. Thomas since the time of Leo XIII. Whatever the details of that history, many are acquainted with its ultimate expression from their student days. Manuals almost as lengthy as the *Summa theologiae*, written in Latin less graceful, played the role of middleman between the student and St. Thomas. To be sure, they all endeavored to proceed *ad mentem Divi Thomae* and to encapsulate the thought of the master. But why, one has to wonder, should Thomas have been treated as if his own writings were lost and only some fragments in the form of quotes, shored against our ruin? The literary form of the Latin manuals insured that intellectual excitement would be kept to a minimum. How many recall somnolent *aulae maximae* where theses were intoned with syllogisms and prosyllogisms following hard upon? Steve Allen used to have a wild skit called the Question Man; you gave him answers and he would provide the questions they resolved. Somehow such manuals did not elicit laughter. The vernacular phase that followed produced textbooks which did little credit to the Latin from which they were derived and sometimes outright violence to the English they professed to be. For all that, there were teachers who taught well with those manuals and there was always a surprising number of textbooks which, once one got used to them, were well done.

I mention these things because memories of them lie behind many expressions of distaste for Thomism. Any word spoken in favor of Thomism is interpreted as a blanket defense of that mountain of manuals written *ad mentem Divi Thomae*, as a claim that all those boring teachers were really excellent. One gathers that for many the Latin formulae took on definitiveness and authority, as if from their very syntax, and later it came almost as a surprise to learn that some vulgarians actually claimed to be doing philosophy in modern languages. With this realization and with the diminution of surprise, it dawned on the victim of the Thomistic tradition that outside the walls the twentieth century was going on apace. But what relation to the issues of the day did his catechetical instruction in philosophy and theology have? There were philosophers in the prime of life or past it who hadn't yet found entrance to the manuals, there to be refuted in a crisp paragraph. One could remember articles entitled *Aliae Sententiae Erroneae circa . . . Refutantur*, but the poor devils impaled there had long since gone to their reward. One had learned where Montesquieu, Kant, Descartes, Hobbes, and Pufendorf had gone wrong, but who in the world were Heidegger and Russell and Wittgenstein? Would it really have been surprising if one had gotten the impression from those manuals that the age of philosophical variants and errors was happily past and that a world-wide consensus had been reached which was being retailed in the manual? In that case, wouldn't one's confidence in the value of those courses waver when he learned that philosophy was a going concern among his contemporaries, that there were hundreds and thousands of philosophers who seemed not to have the faintest inkling of the sort of thing those manuals contained, let alone interest in it? It was just possible that philosophers of the day were doing something else than providing a new catalogue of errors for some future generation of manualists to refute. One could read Kierkegaard and

Husserl and sense that there was something important and interesting being said. Cast forth finally into the twentieth century where no one thinks in Latin, many felt they had been cheated and toyed with during all those years of training. They might turn to Maritain or Pieper or Gilson, of course, but these men were pointing them toward their contemporaries, these men were finding valuable contributions in authors who had never spent fifteen consecutive minutes considering Scholastic philosophy. What then? With disenchantment came rejection and with rejection came the demand for something else, for "relevance." And isn't that the meaning of *aggiornamento?*

In order to understand the profundity of the distaste for Thomism, one has to recognize that what we have been describing was not the experience of a few but an all too common experience. If the picture had been only half as black as it is painted, who could blame those who were subjected to such instruction if they want to throw the whole thing overboard? Surely it is understandable if they are impatient with suggestions that the thing could be tidied up here and there and then it would be all right. They want nothing to do with the Thomistic tradition and they can hardly be expected to be other than dry-eyed at the prospect and hope that it will be eradicated. It is precisely here that I would introduce my variation on the distinction Gilson and Fabro have drawn between Thomas and the Thomistic tradition.

One who feels, as I do, that the Church's wishes with respect to the role St. Thomas should play must be abided by, one who neither wishes nor expects any alteration in those wishes, is not committed to a total or even partial defense of the Thomistic tradition as we have sketched it so blackly above. If that manual interpretation of Aquinas were the only possible response, I would join the chorus of exterminators.

But I refuse to believe that the Church is urging us to continue what has not worked, that She is insisting on an approach to philosophy that has as its usual and predictable result a distaste for and rejection of philosophy. We must learn to distinguish between St. Thomas and the Thomism that has too often obtained in our colleges and seminaries. The latter can be extirpated and cast forth and leave untouched the doctrine of Aquinas himself. If one response has failed, get rid of it; but this cannot be taken to mean that no other response to the stated wishes of the Church is possible.

But now we reach the heart of the matter. When the disenchanted mind turns to contemporary philosophies, a sense of embarrassment can arise at the reminder that the Church has actually expressed Herself on the matter of philosophical instruction. One would prefer to have this mentioned *sotto voce* if at all, concealed as a gaucherie that should not have been committed and will presently be rectified. Who among our contemporaries gives a tinker's dam for such authoritative directives concerning approaches to philosophy? Is not philosophy by its very nature an enterprise based on reason alone? After all, Aquinas himself said that in philosophy authority is the weakest argument; it is no real argument at all, it seems, but a kind of despair of reason. How can philosophy survive except as free inquiry and how is free inquiry possible when there are encyclicals and canon laws which would restrict our philosophical freedom from the outset? All those ecclesiastical documents may seem remnants of a surpassed attitude, something to be discreetly done away with so that the Catholic, like his contemporaries, can philosophize without hindrance and a priori restriction. Here we have the source of that attitude which, depending on one's point of view, can be described as rebellious or truly free and which begs not to be told how to do philosophy. Isn't that demand reasonable? Is it necessary that the Catholic be different from his non-Catholic contemporaries in this? Rather than indoctrination in an alleged true doctrine for which others seem to have disinterest if not contempt, shouldn't there be untrammeled inquiry, a following of the argument whither it goest? Philosophy, it can be objected, does not consist of revealed truths which must be dutifully memorized and assented to because of the authority proposing them. If there are philosophical truths, they must be attained by argument, by appeal to what is accessible in principle to any man, whether or not he has religious faith. Surely that is so, and it is a fact that may easily seem incompatible with the Thomistic tradition. Moreover, it may seem to call into question the source of that tradition, namely the Church's proposing St. Thomas as a guide for our philosophizing. How can the Church dictate on such a matter if philosophy is free inquiry?

I have tried to express an attitude that must be taken seriously into account. One of its assumptions is that, in the normal course of events, philosophy is something that is done without presuppositions; the philosopher is one who begins his task with a *tabula rasa*. What he seeks is evidence and argument and any reference to authority or to truths held on religious belief must be regarded as inappropriate. I shall attempt to show in the sequel that this description of philosophizing does not seem to square with the facts; nevertheless, in doing this, I shall not be out to pooh-pooh the attitude I have been attempting to describe here.

The plan of the essay to follow can now be given. What I am out to show is that a viable and defensible response to the Church's wishes that we take St. Thomas for our philosophical guide can be given. Enough has already been said to make it clear that I have no intention of defending an indefensible traditional response. Before attempting to allay the current fears about any sort of Thomism and before attempting to suggest a possible future Thomism, I want first to remove a more remote impediment to accepting what I have to say. My opening topic is entitled Tradition and Philosophy. However novel and original a philosopher purports to be, this is not the Year One so far as philosophy goes; indeed, most philosophers who are conscious of launching a new movement go to some pains to place what they are doing in relation to what has gone on earlier in the history of philosophy. There is, in short, a sense of tradition in philosophy and we shall want to examine the concept of tradition to see what modifications it introduces into the view that philosophy is something which starts from scratch and without presuppositions.

A second topic, narrower than the first but broader than the specific matter of Thomism, is that of the relation of faith and philosophy. The man of faith comes to philosophy with a number of its big questions already answered; if he truly believes, he has no doubt that God exists, that the soul is immortal, that the world around us is the effect of a transcendent cause. These are not the sum of his certitudes, of course, but they are sufficient to indicate that he is not likely seriously to entertain the possibility that airtight arguments could be devised which would show that for man death is the utter end, that the world is completely self-sufficient, that it is impossible that God exists. How then can the man of faith be a philosopher? It is certainly obvious that if no satisfactory answer to that question can be devised, the further question as to what kind of philosopher he might be will simply not come up.

Finally we shall arrive once more where we began. What in an age of renewal is the role of Thomas Aquinas? This essay is written out of the conviction that the Church has been right all along in directing us to St. Thomas and that She continues to be right. However, since we have excused ourselves from defending the Thomistic tradition, we shall have to sketch the shape of a once and future Thomism. This will be a Thomism which does not exhaust itself in the reading of thirteenth-century texts, though a knowledge of those texts will be an essential component of it. This will not be a Thomism for which everything has been settled in advance; but neither will it be one for which nothing has been or can be settled philosophically. This will be a Thomism which is, by definition, open to every and all instances of philosophizing, but it will not be a dilettantish eclecticism either. The narrator of *The Great Gatsby*, Nick Carroway, describes himself as having been that narrowest of specialists, the well-rounded man. His new attitude is summed up in the observation that the world is much better looked at from a single window after all. For the Thomism I shall commend, Thomas himself may be the window, but what he gives access to is the universe itself, a universe populated not only by things but also by what men have tried to understand of things.

CHAPTER TWO

PHILOSOPHY AND TRADITION

The ambivalence of the concept of tradition resides in the fact that ideas and attitudes are both praised and blamed for being traditional. In the favorable sense, the traditional connotes the hard-won, time-tested achievements handed on from one generation to another. The pejorative sense of the term traditional suggests the pat, accepted, unexamined ballast from the past. Both of these senses have their traditions and this, like barber-shop mirrors, invites the mind to the vertiginous realization that there is a hard-won, time-tested way of regarding tradition as the pat, accepted unquestioned ballast from the past, on the one hand, and, on the other, a pat, accepted, unquestioned way of regarding the traditional as hard-won, time-tested, etc. In short, there are conflicting traditions about the concept of tradition, traditional ways of regarding tradition. Here we want to break the chain and subject both of them to analysis; in doing so, we expect to find some validity in each view. Men are seldom wholly wrong on fundamental issues. And tradition is fundamental to human existence.

Language as Tradition

If we think initially of tradition as the weight of the past upon the present and future, it is difficult to imagine anyone uninfluenced by tradition. The attitudes toward this fact come later and give rise to the conflicting assessments of it we mentioned at the outset. Some choose to accept and praise the fact; others to lament it and to strive to overcome its influence. So regarded, tradition is antecedent to anything like philosophizing. Any human born of parents and thereby introduced into the human community is subject to his elders' influence. Without it he would not survive to the point where he might pass a judgment on the value of the fact. For, in myriad ways, our elders educate us; no man is born human. He becomes so, to the degree that he does, in society. Who can imagine Adam prior to Eve's creation? The easiest thing to forget is our origins and this seems particularly true with those philosophers who seek an absolute, presupposition-less starting point for thought. And yet the only thing more difficult than forgetting we were children is trying to re-member it, to reconstruct from an adult vantage point what it was like, what it entailed. Sometimes it seems that nothing increases the distance and sharpens the difficulty so much as being a parent. But as parents there is no keener delight, per-haps, than that felt when our children begin to speak. It is the fact of language, of the mother tongue, that we want to isolate from the process of becoming human because language above all reveals itself as the vehicle of tradition.

The Greek definition of man can be construed to read that man is the speaking animal and, *Genesis* aside, it is dif-ficult to imagine anyone, any individual, inventing language. A social product, language is what first of all brings us out of our vegetable isolation into the world of men. Language is antecedent to each of us, not as something substantive and thing-like, but as an activity of our elders. I have never seen a satisfactory description of how a child learns to speak, per-haps none could be given, but surely any remotely adequate description would have to lean heavily on the notion of imi-tation. We become like those around us, like our parents, like our siblings, by learning to speak. In some sense of the phrase, language is handed on to us and we must learn to conform to it if we are to be initiated into the world of men.

In order to become what we are, we have to have things handed to us; in order to become a rational animal, an animal who speaks, we have to accept a tradition of communication, of usage, of talk. So far, at least, to be human is to be traditional. A trivial point, to be sure, hardly more than a truism, but the reminder of something this basic must have its ramifications when we turn to less immediate cultural products, particularly when, as is the case with philosophy, language is its proper vehicle. To react against a philosophical tradition, we must employ a language that has been handed down. The language of men is not, of course, what is principally at issue in the conflicting traditions concerning traditions in philosophy but, again, that conflict may not be as separable from this inevitable concession to tradition as the anti-traditionalist might wish.

The instance of tradition we have been looking at is incontestable in its pervasiveness but may seem impertinent to our subject. If we must depend upon our elders in order to learn our mother tongue, it is not speech in general that is involved but talk about various and particular things. Together with our early training, we accept from our elders a vast number of judgments about the way things are and the way they ought to be. These judgments are a kind of a patrimony, a handing on at one term of the relation and, at the other, an acceptance, a receiving. And isn't our reception of that patrimony initially unquestioning? Long before we are aware of doing so, we trust our parents; we take their word for things. Certain ways of looking at the world and ourselves become so familiar they seem merely the expression on the world's face, indeed, part of the furniture of the world. If we say we acquire a *weltanschauung* in child-hood, as we do, this cannot mean that we are presented with some sort of axiomatic system of ideas. The whole business is by way of being a seamless garment and to look for its beginning would be as fruitless as trying to locate with accuracy the commencement of the "age of reason" in the moral sense. If then we begin speaking of tradition in terms of the formation of the child's mind, we find ourselves referring to an englobing, familiar, acquired-in-the-family network of attitudes. And it is all something we accept almost unconsciously. But what has this to do with philosophy?

Well, it can be argued that it has a great deal to do with it, at least when we want to speak about the absolute beginning of philosophy, historically considered. It has long been a commonplace that philosophy began with the Greeks and with them arose out of background of myth. Myth is a difficult concept to lay hold of, to be sure, and there is a tendency to speak of it condescendingly as a phenomenon accompanying the childhood of the race.[1] Perhaps it had its origin in ritual, in the verbalization that accompanied ritual, and then grew into attempts to rationalize primitive rites until it metamorphosed into those familiar tales of gods and divine forces that in some way accounted for cosmic and human events. All this weighed on the minds of those Greeks we call the first philosophers, much as the handed-on judgments and appraisals accepted in childhood weigh on the adult. However gradually it was done, the argument goes, philosophy began when some Greeks began to question the myths, to regard them critically, to withdraw from the earlier acceptance of them. The analogy is clear. A man begins to philosophize, not by accepting what has been handed down, but rather by in some sense reacting against the traditional. Thus, although an attitude of acquiescence to and acceptance of the traditional may be chronologically prior, the philosophical attitude begins there where the mind turns on the traditional and regards it not as an unquestioned deposit of accumulated truths but as a menacing and narrowing threat from the past. Surely something like this is contained in the development of the man who gave philosophy one of its earliest charters: the unexamined life is not worth living.

It is only fitting that we look to Socrates for some clarification of our problem. What do we learn from Socrates in the Platonic dialogues concerning the relation between present and past philosophy, between philosophy and tradition? Did Socrates have a teacher? Was the activity in which Socrates engaged a modification of a going concern or an absolute commencement? It is not uninstructive that we want to answer both yes and no to those last two questions. In the *Phaedo*, Socrates tells us that, as a young man, he applied for instruction to the natural philosophers; he speaks of the influence on him of Anaxagoras' teaching that reason governed the world. It was something he accepted even though he came to feel that Anaxagoras had not put his doctrine to much specific use. If he goes on to speak of his growing dissatisfaction with that early instruction and of his eventual turning away from *cosmos* to *polis*, Socrates adds the balancing note that makes him even more evidently the very type of the philosopher. At one time he subjected himself to a philosophical tradition; later he modified what he had accepted to the point where he could say that he had repudiated his philosophical origins. There is a pattern here which shows up again and again in the great philosophers and, in however modest a way, in the philosophical growth of each of us. Let us look into the elements of the pattern.

We want to examine the process of initiation into philosophy, the process of learning philosophy. Before looking at the reality, however, something must be said of a myth that is often introduced at this point. It used to be said, and rightly, I think, that philosophy begins with wonder, with questions that surge into the mind against the background of our experience of the world. We are assailed by facts that we do not understand so we wonder about them and this wonder can only be assuaged by getting at the reasons for those facts, what is responsible for them, their causes. The points just made become the pigments of which the picture of an individual confronting the world is painted. He poses questions, wordlessly perhaps; at any rate, if he speaks, it is to himself. He solves one question and moves on to another. And so forth. It is possible to become enthralled by this depiction of the solitary, isolated thinker grappling with his problems. But I am calling this picture a myth. I do so because I would hazard the generalization that no one since Pythagoras, perhaps, has ever gone about philosophizing in just that way. What is missing from the picture is an essential ingredient: what that man's predecessors have had to say, the questions they formulated, the answers they proposed. This appeal to one's predecessors has, from almost the beginning of what we call the history of philosophy, been one of the essential ingredients of doing philosophy. It is part and parcel of what I want to call *learning* philosophy.[2]

The men who figure in the history of philosophy have, most of them, called themselves philosophers and, by accepting or laying claim to that title, they are unavoidably comparing themselves and what they are up to with previous men and what they had done. At least with regard to the word "philosophy" they relate themselves to the past, they become part of a tradition. This is not to say that the picture described above depicts nothing in the history of philosophy; as a matter of fact, it tells us something very important about the possibility of progress in philosophy. My point is simply that it is a bad picture of the way any philosopher began doing philosophy. The way he began was as a learner, by putting himself into relation to the past.

The point I am trying to make was made by Aquinas when he distinguished between two ways of coming to know, one of which he called discovery (*inventio*), the other of which he called learning (*disciplina*).[3] In some ultimate sense, the latter depends upon the former, but for every historical philosopher, the former, discovery, has followed upon a period of learning. I want now to go into the meaning of these two kinds of coming to know, their inter-relations and, particularly, the way in which tradition figures in what is called learning.

On Learning Philosophy

Kant summed up the range of philosophy in the following questions: What can I know? What should I do? What can I hope for?[4] What is missing from the picture of the solitary thinker recalled above is the manner in which we are assisted by others, usually our elders, both in the formulation of questions and in the acceptance of certain answers to them. Questions as well as answers are traditional, are handed down. I take this to be factual enough and the fact raises what is, perhaps, the real issue with respect to the role of tradition. That issue has to do with the relationship between tradition and authority. When we become suspicious of tradition, it is because we sense that it induces an unquestioning acceptance of what is said, an acceptance of it simply because it is said. Traditional questions and traditional answers come to us out of a past that we instinctively revere or at least do

not at the outset have the temerity to criticize. The reason
for our acceptance does not seem to be relevant to the substance of what we are accepting, but to englobe and suffuse
it so that it becomes almost awe-inspiring. Throughout our
lives we can be made to pause by remarks that begin with,
"It is well known. . . ." or "Everybody knows. . . ." or
even the less committal, "It is said. . . ." Just as there is
honor among thieves, so the most revolutionary and icono-
clastic types often defer to their fellows in an uncritical fashion. In all its generality, this lack of "the critical spirit" does
not seem destined for any ultimate extinction from the world
of men. Mutual trust will doubtless remain the very glue of
society, its *sine qua non;* the man who insists on clarity and
distinction and certitude *partout* will be boring when he is
not a menace, not the embodiment of the human ideal but a
standing negation of the human situation. And what has
this to do with the learning of philosophy?

Is the role of tradition in learning philosophy a blind acceptance of authority? Aristotle said, in the Latin version,
oportet addiscentem credere: a student must trust his teacher.
It was a remark the medievals liked to quote, but Augustine
said we do not send our children to school to learn what
the teacher knows. It is important to see that they are both
right, that the trust and belief Aristotle advocates must not
only give way, but is teleologically ordered to, the autonomous seeing Augustine demands. Pieper has put it this way:
"All tradition is something preliminary and provisional. Tradition in an absolute sense, tradition that can never be replaced through the progress of science cannot be imagined
unless it be assumed that there are *tradita* which by their very
nature cannot be tested by experience and argument, cannot
be verified."[5] Teaching, as Aquinas speaks of it, is a discourse which may for a time be accepted out of trust in the

teacher but should be so presented that that kind of extraneous reason for accepting it is easily replaced. What enables us to overcome the authoritative basis for acceptance is acquaintance with, advertence to, the things spoken of as well as recourse to what we know prior to subjecting ourselves to instruction. However social our existence, Aquinas observes that each of us comes instinctively to know certain things about the world and about ourselves, things which it would be irrational to doubt and impossible to reject. For him, as for the plain man, the so-called principle of contradiction is not in the first instance a rule of logic but a fact about whatever is. Such truths, however tricky-sounding their verbal formulation, however difficult their analysis, however complex their defense—all of which comes later—provide criteria for the learner which make him wary of any remark which violates those truths. Nothing can be deduced from them, but they are a test of the acceptability of statements which also claim to be about the things that are. Aquinas' reference to such immediate, self-evident truths, which stand for any man's awareness of inescapably obvious features of reality, makes it clear that there is built into the very process whereby we listen to what others have to say a principle of critical acceptance or rejection. One who accepts only because it has been said, because it is traditional, is accepting on authority, on someone's say-so, and if that attitude is terminal, he is short-circuiting the process of learning.

We have pointed out that Aquinas distinguished two ways of coming to know, being taught and discovering by oneself. Of the two, it is the second that is the sign of a stronger mind; if we had to choose between the original thinker, the man who alights for the first time on a truth we find compelling, and the man who knows everything that his predecessors knew, we would no doubt select the first. But, in doing so, we would be wrong to think that the learned man lacks intellectual autonomy. This he cannot do if, as we have said, he has *learned* what his predecessors knew. For, if he has learned, he no longer accepts because it was held by his predecessors but rather because he has come to see that such-and-such is so. Tradition as authority fulfills its role by a flourish and exit.

We must now make an effort to ward off a misunderstanding our discussion of the learning of philosophy may encourage. The reader could easily think that the situation we have been describing when we spoke of learning philosophy is best exemplified, even solely exemplified, by someone sitting in a philosophy classroom or curled up with the first book he has ever drawn from the philosophy shelf of his father's library. In academic discussions over the years there is a remark I have heard again and again from teachers of philosophy when they are describing the difficulties of their craft. The college student, they will say, has had some prior introduction to history and mathematics and science, to nearly every other curricular offering, but philosophy is for him something wholly new. That remark, it seems to me, could scarcely be more wrong and it is symptomatic of what has happened to philosophy in these last days. Surely it makes a good deal more sense to say that of any course a student could possibly take none connects more surely with his spontaneous thinking, his pre- and extra-academic thinking, than does—or should—his first course in philosophy. Recall those questions Kant said summed up the task of the philosopher and try to think of them as marking off the domain of an expert, some esoteric technician whose ways and words are hopelessly removed from the common world of men. Kant's questions are human questions, questions most men most likely have posed themselves, in some form or another, and have had posed for them, in one form or another, from the dawn of their recognizably human lives. Wouldn't it be better and more salutary to regard philosophy as the attempt to do well what we can scarcely help doing one way or the other if we are men at all? Mortimer Adler has made this point recently and forcibly by reminding us of those first-order questions which are the professional philosopher's link with that plain man he loves to appeal to in argument, the plain man he was himself and, it is devoutly to be wished, basically remains.[6] When philosophy loses that nexus with its origin in the inquiry of any mind awake to reality it becomes fantastic and a menace, fully deserving of a swift kick from the Johnsonian boot. There is no doubt, of course, that in the process of trying to do well what each man willy-nilly does, the professional philosopher is forced to ask Adler's second-order questions, that even in his elaboration of first-order, spontaneous questions, his attempts at solution could boggle the plain man. But whenever a philosopher coaxes us to hang on to the brush because he is taking away the ladder which leads back to common experience, the gravity we may be induced momentarily to feel will certainly and ignominiously ground us.

What I am suggesting is that we begin the study of philosophy long before we begin "the study of philosophy." We know all kinds of things for sure before we commence that formal study and, besides, our minds are chock full of opinions, theories, arguments we have taken on from that bountiful parent, tradition. There is no single inventory of the furniture of a mind which comes to the formal study of philosophy, in a classroom or by reading a book, but whatever the particular inventory there will likely always be two main classifications of it: what is really known, reasons that truly found what is held, reasonable opinions, on the one hand, and, on the other, all kinds of beliefs whose only warrant is familiarity, their repetition by ourselves and others. The latter may be the common assumptions of a given time, elements of a *zeitgeist*, the myths of an age as, in our own time, Toulmin suggests, science is our controlling myth.[7] What we would expect from the formal study of philosophy is a progressive separation of these two kinds of mental furniture, a questioning of the previously unquestioned, a testing of what we think are reasoned beliefs. There is no one way to do this, of course, and the variety of methods is not an unequivocal blessing. Perhaps the least safe guides at this point are philosophers who glory in the appellation "critical," who suggest that the criterion for this sifting is not something brought to philosophy and constantly alluded to in its critical progression, but an asset to be gained from philosophy, to be acquired. There are legitimate senses of an intra-philosophical starting point but in the most basic of senses the starting point of formal philosophy is brought to it. The study of philosophy may create a new awareness of what one already knew before beginning that study but when it pretends to confer the beginnings of thought something has gone radically wrong.

The foregoing looks like an appeal to common sense and, in a sense, it is. The trouble with common sense is not, as Descartes said, that everyone is cocksure he has an adequate supply, but rather that, as a phrase, it smudges the difference between what we really know without the aid of others or have with the aid of others come to know and, what is quite different, the merely customary, familiar, and accepted. The proponents of common sense would like it to be made up only of the former; its opponents suggest it consists only of the latter. If it comprises both, the critique of common sense will be the questioning of the merely familiar by appeal to what is really known. How in practice can we tell which is which? The answer to that could be phrased in terms of a basic belief in the capacity of the human mind, but that sounds rather exalted. Perhaps it would be better to suggest the following rule of thumb. Some of the things we maintain simply because they are familiar have only to be articulated to exhibit the fact that we have no good reason for maintaining them; other beliefs of the same sort may resist being nudged for reasons, but if we consider what it would be like if they were not so, our view of the world may seem at first surprisingly altered but still inhabitable. For example, the suggestion that we know a lot of things about the world for sure, both facts and reasoned facts, without appeal to the scientific method, may seem shocking at first.[8] But when we reflect that we really haven't the least idea yet what the scientific method is, or indeed any reason to suppose it is some one procedure, the shock can give way to the recognition that it was ridiculous to think otherwise, however implicitly. We may have become so responsive to "scientific" as an adjective which commends and commands that we have made of it a mantle to cover whatever nudity. Needless to say, a lifetime could be spent in this critical appraisal of the furniture of our mind and there would still be a good deal left untouched. Furthermore, though there are times in our life, and in the history of philosophy, when the impulse is felt to send packing any belief which does not have absolute and incontestable grounding in what is evident and irreproachable, we come eventually to see that such beliefs have a way of returning from exile, that we cannot do without them, that—and here is the dark night of the rationalistic soul—by far the majority of our notions have only varying degrees of a garden variety of probability to commend them.

However nostalgic we may sometimes feel for a rationalistic paradise where thoughts form a vast concatenation presided over by certitude and clarity and distinction, we learn, if learn we must, that that mathematical ideal is largely irrelevant to human knowledge, perhaps even to mathematics itself. Not everything can be proved or, perhaps, we come to see that the proof of more than pudding is in the eating. *Gustate et videte*, then, and *de gustibus non disputandum est.* There are lots of things in heaven and earth and philosophy can be made commodious enough not to deserve Hamlet's shushing of Horatio.

The Advantages of Tradition

We began our discussion of tradition by citing the instance of language; if the learning of our mother tongue is the acceptance of something handed down and if to be a man is to be an animal who speaks, tradition is essential to human existence. That seemed to load the case in favor of tradition; indeed it became unclear that there was any alternative to it, until we moved on to speak specifically of learning philosophy. Recalling Socrates, we introduced the notion that philosophy involves a critical note insofar as it sees its function as questioning the traditional, the familiar, what everybody knows. This suggestion has the merit of describing philosophical activity in its social context, as a man's response not only to the world but to what men have had to say about the world. While emphasis must be given to this critical function of philosophy, insofar as it can be described as a critique of common sense we found it advisable to distinguish among the contents of common sense. Furthermore, we suggested that in learning philosophy from another, there are positive advantages. It is this suggestion we want now to explore.

Learning as the acceptance of what is handed on, coming to know with the aid of a teacher, is an instance of tradition that need involve only two generations, at least for purposes of discussion. We will turn later to tradition as involving a plurality of generations, even a whole civilization or culture.

I suppose that anyone who speaks of one man's being instructed by another, whether this be in a formal or informal sense, will want to describe and even justify this ineluctable part of being human by saying that the instructed is a recipient, that there are advantages in his situation which are merely particularizations of the advantages of living in the society of his fellows. We have already suggested that we are led by our elders to ask certain questions, about the world and about ourselves, and that in most cases a solution comes hard upon the formulation of a question. If we should approach this situation by imagining, first of all, how we could lament its existence, it will be easier later to show its advantages. When people wax eloquent about the task of the "educator" (a term which may seem abstract enough but, in the escalation of the jargon, soon cedes to "educationist"), they speak of molding young minds, forming the young, leaving their impress on the supposedly malleable mind of youth, etc. What if it were objected that this is tyrannical, that the fault Augustine cited is not merely an adventitious result, but the intended and predictable result of one man's presuming to teach another? The teacher, the objection would run, is simply imposing his ideas on his victim, making another's mind over in the image of his own, training, directing, limiting. I am trying so to express this possible objection that it is clear that teaching is regarded as an assault on the freedom of the taught. The word that sums this up is, of course, indoctrination. One could easily conclude from the considerations that would accompany an expanded form of the objection I am sketching that any positive content of teaching, any effort to solve the questions raised in this relation between generations, is an imposition of one set of personal views on another man who has the right to form his own equally personal views. It may be all right to lead others to ask questions, but we must avoid like sin the impulse to give answers. What the objection would do with the suggestion that conveying certain questions rather than others is its own kind of limitation, I don't know.

It would be easy to lampoon the objection, so easy in fact that one might seriously doubt that anyone had ever lodged it. But men have held the view involved in this objection and, while I shall not document this, I am certain I am addressing a real position. Even if it were not currently represented, however, it could be regarded as a meaningful possibility hinted at by Augustine. It is meaningful because it is not utterly absurd. Consider the implications of Augustine's curt remark: we do not send our sons to school to learn what the teacher knows. Surely he is right in saying that the point of learning is not that one mind might discover what another mind thinks, just as such. There are all kinds of situation where we listen to another simply to hear what he (or, more likely, she) has to say, what she thinks, how she regards this or that.[9] But, generally speaking, we would want to distinguish learning in the strong sense from such situations. In certain polar instances of it, we might want to say that the person of the teacher is a vanishing element in the process of learning; at the opposite pole, the teacher as this person assumes a far greater importance. But through the spectrum, whatever the degree of personal importance the teacher may have, insofar as one is learning he is not simply learning what another thinks just insofar as it is what another thinks. The objection we have mentioned above may seem to suggest that someone might say to us that snow is green and we react by recording that Snodgrass thinks that snow is green. But normally, of course, we would want to know why he thinks so. Say we asked and he begins with trembling voice to speak of an unhappy childhood when every impulse was stifled, every instance of independent thought repressed. We may begin to feel, as we edge toward an exit, that we have gained some understanding of why he made the statement, but the reasons in play could hardly be said to have anything intrinsic to do with what the statement, snow is green, means. I am trying to arrive at the truism that the learning process is best considered in terms of the following paradigm. We are told that the intrinsic angles of a plane triangle are equal to two right angles and then are shown, in terms of what is being talked about, reasons for accepting the statement. Now, afterward, we might of course résumé the whole business by saying that Professor Snodgrass thinks that the intrinsic angles of a plane triangle are equal to two right angles because of this and that. We could then be asked, "Yes, but what do you think?" There is a whole range of possible answers. "I don't know if *I* would want to say that." "I'm not sure." "I couldn't care less." "I think the opposite is true." "Sometimes but not always." Often enough, if our reply is of a certain kind, we will be asked reasons for maintaining what we maintain, reasons that can be grasped and appraised by one who knows what we are talking about. Say we give our reason and are told, "But that is Snodgrass's reason." Wouldn't we want to say that it is and is not his, just as it is and is not ours? If no one held the reasons in question, they would of course belong to no one, but if they are held they are not held as personal views in some private sense but as judgments borne out by what we are talking of.

It is embarrassing to be dwelling on points as obvious as these, but they do connect with our problem and there is some advantage in recalling the indisputable when one engages in dispute. The suite of truisms just mentioned enables us to add some more. When we learn from another, in the sense of learning which interests us here, the sense which connects with the formal study of philosophy, our instructor draws our attention, not to himself, but to what he is talking about. Moreover, we have independent access to what he is talking about. It may well be that what he says is the occasion for our attending to what he is talking about, but there is no strong sense in which he could be said to confer awareness of what we are then aware of. Further, what he then goes on to say about the objects to which we are attending has as its measure and criterion those objects—and not merely what we, in some private sense, think of those objects. This has as its corollary the suggestion that, in principle at least, we could, by attending to those objects independently of the help of others, come to see what, thanks to instruction, we are being led to see. That is why Aquinas speaks of the teacher as an artist who imitates nature; that is, the teacher tries to get us to perform under his guidance the steps we might have performed without it. It will be appreciated why Aquinas held that learning and discovery bear on the same matter. We are now in a position to list rather summarily the advantages which have been ascribed to learning, to the acceptance of what is handed down by the teacher.

In principle, whatever one man knows about a range of objects is knowable by others. What may have been come upon in a hit-or-miss manner can be conveyed economically to others; we can come to see rather rapidly what it may have taken our elders a very long time to discover. There is a good deal of talk nowadays about the logic of discovery since this has once more been freed from the logic of codification, systematization, doctrine.[10] The original optimism of a Descartes or Leibniz that men could be taught the art of discovery has given way to the realization that discovery, as it has historically occurred (although even the facts of discovery do not yield themselves easily and unambiguously to investigation), is not some one thing. There is no formula for it and its students fall inevitably back on words like genius and insight and creativity, words which point but do not explain. The foregoing should indicate that, while the learning process involves an eventual seeing on the part of the learner which is independent of historical statements about Professor Snodgrass and his alma mater, this process is best kept distinct from discovery in the strong sense. Now the advantages of learning from another are usually expressed in terms of more than two generations, say Snodgrass and spiritual *fils*. So, too, tradition is usually reserved to speak of a handing down involving many generations. One can see the picture that will be drawn. Over many generations there is an accumulation of knowledge; what is known is passed on, new discoveries are made and add to the deposit of knowledge and together with what has been received is passed on to the next crop of learners. And so on. In terms of this picture, the thought of someone beginning from scratch and attempting to do in the brief span of his lifetime a significant portion of what preceding generations have done can only be depressing. All honor to discovery, the proponents of intellectual tradition would say, but thank God each man is not held to discover everything. Just as we would think it odd to provide children with a fourth- or fourteenth-century map of the world and let them find out for themselves its inadequacy, so generally with learning we ought to hand on whatever has been gained, the present state of this discipline or that. Against the background of tradition, true as opposed to apparent and repetitious discoveries can be made which will contribute to the advance of human knowledge. We are reminded that a schoolboy today may, thanks to being taught, rank higher than a genius of bygone days and we are induced to feel humility by imagining the learning of some child a thousand years hence.

The picture is undeniably an attractive one, but of what is it a picture? In our own times, it is only in the realm of the sciences, and with some diffidence even there, that this picture of a steady advance of human knowledge is invoked. What possible application can it have to art or to human behavior or, and here for us is the rub, to philosophy? Is there progress and cooperation in philosophy anywhere near comparable to that in science which can justify the application of the following to philosophy? "The master-pupil relation is but an instance and a facet of a wider set of institutions, providing for mutual reliance and mutual discipline among scientists, by which the practice of discovery is ordered and the premises of science are fostered and developed."[11] If there is any such accumulation of philosophical truths which are generally recognized to be such and which function as the springboard of present inquiry, it is clear that few philosophers have heard of it. What we find over and over again in the history of philosophy is a valiant effort on an individual's part to begin the process, to lay the first foundations for such progress. With the advent of what we call science, the problem has become particularly aggravated, for philosophers could look to the progress of science as to a model of their own aspirations for the future of philosophy. As recently as Husserl, as recently as the *International Encyclopedia of Unified Science*, efforts were made to put philosophy, for the first time, on firm foundations, to make of it a science in the strict sense.[12] It is not the aspiration that is new: it is as old as philosophy. It is not the sense that one has managed to bring it off that is novel: that, too, is as old as philosophy. What is striking is the inability on the part of philosophers to convince their fellows that they have managed to come up with something which is firm, which will stand the ravages of time and compel assent from those who follow the argument. In short, the history of philosophy, when it is approached with the picture of an ever-increasing body of commonly held doctrine, must appear incredibly messy, a story of thwarted hopes, of both mild and gigantic delusions, a catalogue of mistakes and errors.

If that assessment of the history of philosophy were true, what possible justification could there be for commending the learning of philosophy? Presumably there is nothing positive to learn. We could, to be sure, fall back on the negative benefit of not beginning *ab ovo*: it is possible to learn to avoid past errors. Philosophical documents could still function as warnings and caveats. There is another suggestion, more dire still, and that is that we have surpassed the time when what was called philosophy is justifiable. What if we are living in a post-philosophical age? In the title of a vastly entertaining little book, the question is formulated *Pourquoi des philosophes?*[13] If philosophy has never succeeded in coming to be hitherto, is there really any need for it now? The suggestion is, in a word, that our realization of the past unsuccess of philosophy should prompt us, not to try to do well what our predecessors failed to do at all, but to resist the temptation to do philosophy. One thing at least is certain; in our own day the regnant views concerning the nature of philosophy have little in common with older views: furthermore, the influential types of philosophy are quite clearly defined in terms of the pervasive and undeniable reality of the sciences. If it is to be justified at all, philosophy must stake out its claim in such a way that it clearly takes into account the achievements of science. In its way, that is the very mark of philosophy since Descartes, but today it has come to be accepted without question that philosophy must define itself as over against the sciences. Given the fact of the sciences, what is the nature of, or even the need for, philosophy; what could the objects and method of philosophy possibly be? To view the matter in any other way is an anachronism that cannot command serious attention.

Philosophers and Philosophy

We began with the intention of discussing the relation between philosophy and tradition and the way was fairly smooth so long as we restricted talk of tradition to rather common features of man's social existence; when we shifted to the level of learning, of being taught, the discussion could once more proceed and it was possible to indicate the advantages of being taught, at least so long as our examples were mathematical. The moment we attempted to apply the description of the cumulative nature of knowledge and the way the learner benefits from this to philosophy and the learning of philosophy the roof fell in. Right now, we seem to have reached a point where we must say that, however inevitable and advantageous tradition may be in the life of man, and even in his intellectual life when we think of the sciences, there can be no meaningful talk of a tradition in philosophy. Indeed, we seem to have to take seriously the suggestion that any cogent excuse for indulging in philosophy is presently absent, that philosophy is a feature of more primitive times and that it has therefore been surpassed.

Further progress can nonetheless be made in our discussion if only we will make a somewhat shocking assumption. Mention has been made of the fact that nowadays philosophers must perforce justify what they are doing in the light of the success of the sciences. If there is a cumulative tradition of knowledge anywhere, it would appear to be in the sciences and philosophers, envious and respectful of this fact, have studied the nature of science to find the clue to that success. Some have been enthralled by pure mathematics and have longed for a *mathesis universalis*, a common method at present exemplified only in mathematics which might be isolated and described and then applied to non-mathematical questions in the hope that they, like mathematical ones, can be brought to a definitive solution. Others look to physical science for the base from which they can proceed to formulate the general method. The dream is of philosophy as a strict science. It could be objected that there are many philosophers who look to science, not as a model, but as the limiting other-than-philosophy, that which philosophy is not and whose methods and devices are inappropriate to philosophy. This is true. But where these two attitudes coalesce is in their conviction that philosophy must be understood as over and against science. It is not merely that philosophy is more than science or less than science but that science is not philosophy. But why should we assume that this is so? Why should we regard philosophy as a mode of thought whose territory has been progressively invaded and occupied by something alien called science? When we make that assumption, we are inexorably led, if we want to save philosophy, to search for a distinctive area for philosophy, some territory not yet or perhaps in principle incapable of being occupied by science. Further, we seek some peculiar and distinctive method which will set philosophy off from science. What has led to the making of this familiar—I am tempted to say, traditional—assumption?

It need not be cynical to suggest that career motives have been somewhat responsible for the quest outlined in the preceding paragraph. Mortimer Adler, in the book already referred to, goes to great pains to distinguish the method of philosophy from those of science and history. Why? He wants to make philosophers respectable in present-day society. Who are the objects of his concern? When we see that he is concerned for those who occupy positions as professors of philosophy (or as researchers in philosophical institutes), we need not regard his book as a kind of Luddite gesture on behalf of job security. Rather, we should ask why academic divisions of labor should be accepted in an unquestioning way. We must ask how it has come about that a small portion of academe, members of a department in one college, have come to be distinguished from their fellows by their insistence on the title, philosopher. Rather than say that the sciences have usurped a goodly amount of the traditional territory of philosophy, we could perhaps more correctly say that a small group of those who are engaged in the pursuit of knowledge have usurped the title philosopher and in the process shrunk the territory originally assigned to philosophy.

This suggestion could be greeted with the objection that, to follow it through, would entail appeal to some Pickwickian sense of "philosophy" and "philosopher," but the obvious countercharge is that, viewed in a broad perspective, it is the contemporary philosopher who is wont to use these terms in odd ways. What precisely happened when physics ceased to be called the philosophy of nature? What precisely happened when the academic degree of those engaged in the study of nature became Doctor of Science rather than the traditional Doctor of Philosophy? Was this a verbal move and, if not, what exactly was it? I want to suggest that a good deal of the malaise and mystery will begin to lift from philosophers' reflection on their task when they admit that it is not the territory of philosophy that has shrunk with the success of science; all that has shrunk is the agreed-upon range of the term, philosophy, and what is left has been increasingly described in ways which are silly, pompous, imperial, or fruitless. What would be lost by saying that, with respect to our knowledge of nature, questions which were once asked and not very successfully answered by men who called themselves philosophers are now being asked, even though formulated differently, by men we have chosen not to call philosophers? One could retort by asking what would be gained by the admission. What would clearly be gained, I think, is a cessation of esoteric attempts to define philosophy as something at all costs different from and other than science. Rather than having won a verbal victory, we would be spared the continuation of basically verbal battles. We would be spared the quest for odd objects for philosophical inquiry and stranger descriptions of the method of approach to those objects. Retention of the broad notion of philosophy maintained by Plato and Aristotle would enable us to see that the knowledge one in quest of wisdom wants includes what is now called science; given the importance and interest of science for the seeker of wisdom, there is no good reason to deny the epithet "philosophical" to science. The quest for wisdom may involve asking questions the sciences do not ask, it may involve reflecting on the sciences, but this does not require us to deny that the sciences are components of philosophy. Literary criticism, reflection on art, does not require a special expertise unavailable in Departments of English; reflection on the nature of and method of science does not require appeal to members of the Department of Philosophy. Philosophy is simply not some specialty over and against the other specialties in the modern university. By aspiration at least philosophy is what binds together the various knowledges and methods scattered throughout the university. Etymologically, philosophy connotes a teleological ordering of all available knowledge to the asking of ultimate questions about the world and man. These ultimate questions are not distinct from but in continuity with the questions which constitute the various activities in academe. Viewed in this way, it becomes clear that the fruitful asking of ultimate questions cannot be the work of those who are in ignorance of what is being done throughout the university, the intellectual community. If philosophy aims at going beyond science to wisdom, it ought to be quite clear that one cannot go beyond what he does not know.

I am suggesting that philosophy be taken to be a name which covers all academic pursuits insofar as these are regarded as prerequisite for dealing with ultimate questions. No one can handle ultimate questions who is not well grounded in the various academic disciplines; therefore, these must be regarded as constituents of philosophy and not merely propaedeutic to it. What the various disciplines, regarded as constituents of philosophy, are propaedeutic to is the sapiential view, the culminating questions. The effort to treat the natural and social sciences, aesthetics, and so forth as other than philosophy has led to the identification of philosophy with a methodological activity, a meta-discipline, or as exclusively an ontology or metaphysics. The first understanding of its nature dictates that philosophy has no subject matter, at least no first-order subject matter; in the second, it has a subject matter so esoteric and incommunicable that efforts to describe it in isolation from its dependence on the sciences lead to obfuscating and incantatory claims. Much better, I am suggesting, to realize that most philosophical questions are treated nowadays by men we have chanced not to call philosophers and that those who do claim to be philosophers must recognize this fact and proceed to "save" philosophy by once more extending its scope even though this has the paradoxical look of saying that most of philosophy is "non-philosophy." For what finally have we gained by ceasing to regard, as Plato and Aristotle did, mathematics and natural science as parts of philosophy? Surely we have nothing to lose by reclaiming that ancient view. The more commodious outlook is infinitely preferable to attempts that can be likened to speaking of a train in abstraction from all cars other than the engine—or the caboose.

Should it need emphasizing, the new—or older—usage I am recommending would not have as its purpose or effect any flattering of the sciences; its purpose is to induce a becoming modesty in those of us who still lay claim to the title of philosopher. Its advantage for our present purposes is that we are prevented from asking what *the* method of philosophy is, what philosophy as something utterly other than science would be. When we recognize that there is much more to philosophy than is done in Departments of Philosophy, questions about the teaching and learning of philosophy can never be as simple as they may initially appear. However, with respect to the question of a cumulative tradition in knowledge, we could then say that while this is not unarguably present in all areas of philosophy, it is present in some areas of philosophy, areas like physics, logic, mathematics, etc. In other parts of philosophy, parts identified with philosophy by Mortimer Adler and too many others, matters are more problematical. Now, in what follows, I shall principally concern myself with what is taken to be covered by the more restricted use of "philosophy," but I hope that this will not be read as in any way diminishing the importance of our suggestion as to the true range of philosophy. Of course many philosophical questions, in the restricted sense of the adjective, fall within the range of what today we call not philosophy but science. For example, the question, "What is man?" need not be regarded as a philosophical addendum to biology and anthropology and psychology—but of course this recognition may amount to a critique of certain views of biology and anthropology and psychology. The narrowing of philosophy, by philosophers, has doubtless had deleterious effects on disciplines other than "philosophy." That is why, perhaps, interesting differences about the nature of philosophy are seldom to be found in the positions of professional philosophers; rather they are found in operative views on the unity of knowledge within the university, in the area called, alas, philosophy of education. I say alas because "philosophy" has become synonymous with such meta-views regarded as distinct from and other than the things which are bound together.

Language and Philosophy

At the beginning of this chapter, in preparation for treating the question of philosophy and tradition, we made the point that the fact of language is a powerful instance of tradition. Now, having come, I hope, some distance from that opening consideration, having seen something of the unhappy effects of our distinctly modern and really rather recent shrinking of philosophy into some sort of ineffectual competitor of science, we want to ask about the role of language as the vehicle for conveying philosophical knowledge. If language with its meanings and usages involves ordinary discourse in a necessary deference to tradition, we want to ask whether language has meanings gathered from successful efforts to ask and answer questions which go beyond the workaday world. We are suggesting, by posing the issue in this fashion, both a distinction between uses of language and a connection between those two uses. How does the teacher lead one who knows how to use language in an ordinary way to ask and answer questions which have traditionally been called philosophical? The preceding section indicates that our problem could be treated by asking about the proper way to teach physics, biology, economics, political science, or mathematics. Any of these disciplines could, on the basis of the previous section, be regarded as parts of philosophy. Actually we shall be proceeding in terms of considerations so general that such divisions of knowledge need not be explicitly alluded to.

The proper instrument of the teacher is language. That ringing phrase can be attributed to Aquinas and it should strike us first as having a false tone. We think of the master plumber teaching his apprentice, and language, apart from an occasional illustrative expletive, may seem to be a small and even dispensable part of his instruction. We think of a backfield coach teaching a quarterback how to "hand off" artfully and with the maximum of deception. In principle the process could come off with a dumb coach or a deaf quarterback: the coach *shows* the boy how to do it. Aquinas' claim obviously does not apply to every activity we would call teaching or instruction. Nor need we think that what is involved is some latter-day extension of the use of the terms in question. Aquinas must have had in mind a certain range of uses of "teaching," perhaps even a controlling instance of teaching, in virtue of which his remark made sense. The words he uses in connection with his assertion are *doctrina* and *disciplina*. We have already seen that, for him, not every instance of coming to know is learning or *disciplina;* he reserves that term for coming to know with the aid of a teacher. But not every teacher uses language in order to fulfill his function. The paradigmatic instance of learning for Aquinas, as for the Greeks, is mathematics. This is embarrassing, of course, because when we speak of the language of mathematics we have the sense of employing a metaphor; we seem to be suggesting that the symbolism of mathematics is like the "natural" language and, of course, unlike it.[14] Although mathematics would seem to be his paradigmatic instance of teaching and learning, the notions are broadened to include all questions which bear on the way things are when solutions to these questions are achieved as the term of mental activity as opposed to crafts, techniques, and so forth. Questions bearing on nature, the coming to be of things in the world, change and time and purpose, of the distinction of living and non-living bodies, questions having to do with the course of the planets, the nature of man, his difference from other cosmic entities and his destiny, human society, etc.—these very broad matters indicate the range of human inquiry and, at the beginning, with the Greeks, the term philosophy was used to embrace them all. Its defining note, to be sure, has not yet been struck. The wisdom to which all knowledge was ultimately ordered—and it was precisely its ordination to wisdom that made other knowledge deserving of being called philosophical—involved asking questions about the possibility of, indeed the necessity for, a reality different from and explanatory of the real things of our more immediate experience. The destiny of philosophy, for the Greeks, was, in short, theology: what man can know of the divine. Now, as we indicated earlier, while one must maintain that in principle a man might ask some or most or perhaps all of these questions without prompting from others, the normal course of events is such that one is induced to ask them by the influence of others. Furthermore, not all these questions await the formal study of philosophy for their asking; that formal study presupposes that we recognize basic questions, that we already feel more or less at home with them. That formal study relies on our tendency to want to give an account of experience, to ask *why* of things that happen. Long before philosophy began, such questions were asked and various accounts given by way of an answer to them; philosophy begins under the influence of those accounts just as today the study of philosophy begins under the influence of antecedent attitudes, whether secular or religious. That is why, from the very outset, philosophy is at least implicitly critical of accepted accounts. In brief, then, philosophy begins by presupposing a natural tendency to seek an account of experience, a natural tendency which is encouraged by society and assuaged in part by its traditional accounts. As a societal effort, these antecedents involve as well a language in which the questions and traditional answers are framed. It is by employing that language, which is the vehicle and repository of "common sense," that philosophy begins its work, a work which is at once critical and constructive. At the outset philosophy need not deal with unusual questions; in any case, it is not odd objects or questions which constitute the move to formal philosophy. What takes place is a shift in the method and quality of handling familiar questions. It is here that the notion of science (*episteme:* knowing in a strong sense) was introduced. As an ideal, science or *episteme* received a rather definitive formulation in Aristotle's *Posterior Analytics*, but at the same time Aristotle corrects an impression Plato gave, namely, that any philosophical question, if it could be answered at all, was answerable in the same way. The notion of science or *episteme* became a variable one, not only because of diverse subject matters but also because of degrees of approximation to the ideal. Thus it becomes impossible to speak of philosophical method as of something unique, univocal, and unchanging.

The kind of beginning we are attributing to philosophy now leads to the expectation that there will be a kind of sameness to philosophical questions. If formal philosophy is an attempt to do well the kind of thinking men more or less instinctively do, a questioning which initially arises out of a practical involvement in the world, that very continuity with respect to object and language with the pre-philosophical should lead to fairly broad agreement as to the range of those questions and, perhaps, a kind of progress in handling them. It is to this expectation that we now turn.

Philosophia perennis

When Aristotle looked over the work of his predecessors, he had a way of sifting that work for elements which he could then examine for the meaning and direction they implied for future intellectual labor. The elements thus sifted out of what his predecessors had said often have a surprising look to them, losing as they do in the process many of the characteristics that were theirs in their original habitat. Nor could Aristotle be more explicit in letting us know that what governs his activity is not what his predecessors might have meant, not even what they actually said, in a limited sense: he is, so to speak, looking for a truth hidden beneath the surface of the opinions and arguments and positions that had come down to him.[15] Often there are tensions in a man's theory not wholly explicable in terms of what is explicit in the theory. What is most remarkable about Aristotle's work as an historian of philosophy is the way in which he sees reality as the measure of what has been said about it. Thus he will point out that his predecessors said certain things as if compelled by the truth of being. In short, it is as if, despite idiosyncrasies and predilections, despite the favorite themes and outlook of this sect or that school, reality asserts itself in what men have had to say in dealing with certain questions. The procedure suggests, of course, that a dialectical shakedown of philosophical problems and positions, no matter how opposed and other they may superficially seem, will have as its result the discernment of common truths. When the whole history of philosophy is looked upon in this way, we arrive at what has come to be called the "Perennial Philosophy."

The notion of a perennial philosophy transcends, because it accounts for, the scandal of philosophical diversity, of philosophical pluralism. Whatever the causes of that diversity —and, while surely uncountable, such causes could range from the trivial and absurd to the profound—the diversity is interesting only because it masks a discoverable unity. Notice that one who holds that there is a kind of perennial philosophy which survives and thrives in the conflict of positions does not thereby come out for the extinction of diversity. First of all, however desirable the doing away of diversity may sometimes seem, it is unrealistic to expect its disappearance, unrealistic because of the nature of some of the sources of that diversity. Second, and more seriously, the believer in a perennial philosophy will usually regard it as in some way the product of philosophical diversity. If this is so, no one philosophy could be the perennial philosophy even when one philosophy is considered to be the privileged locus, custodian, and discoverer (or rediscoverer) of the perennial philosophy. To point out that one who holds there is a perennial philosophy which is the product of philosophical pluralism and further holds that nonetheless one philosophy plays a privileged role in the discovery of perennial philosophy seems to point to a certain smugness. If this be smugness, however, smugness is an essential trait of the philosopher.

Let me expand that enigmatic remark. Every philosopher feels an adequate judge, at least in principle, of anything that goes by the name of philosophy—and of much else besides. It would be difficult, though not wholly impossible,[16] to find a philosopher who holds that there are any number of truly alternative ways of doing what he is doing which are of equal value to his own. For one thing, explicitly to hold that is to adopt a point of view other than "one's own view" from which it and others are regarded and said to be mutually compatible and equally defensible. Is that higher viewpoint compatible with its contradictory? A given philosopher may in fact be indifferent to much of what other philosophers do or have done, but so soon as he relates what he is interested in to the rest he reveals the conviction that he is adequately equipped, in virtue of what he has done, to pass an implicit judgment on the whole of philosophy. What I am fumbling toward is this. One might want to oppose the notion of perennial philosophy by introducing with warm fanfare and the appropriate diffidence the notion of philosophical pluralism. That is, while some might argue for an essential unity in philosophical diversity, others may profess to be perfectly satisfied with that diversity, a diversity spoken of now in a commending way by calling it pluralism. But what is the essential difference between the philosophical "perennialist" and the philosophical "pluralist"?

One is tempted to say that no philosopher can be a pluralist.[17] Certainly he cannot be if by this is meant that he maintains that two views on the same matter, views which profess to say the same sort of thing about that same matter, are equally and indisputably true. But of course pluralism as a theory comes in precisely when men begin to despair of indisputable truths. Let us say then that the pluralist is one who is wary of rejecting any effort to deal with a given question in favor of another effort. To make our point quickly, doesn't this attitude of the pluralist look a lot like the attitude of one who holds there is a perennial philosophy? They are both views about the value of the diversity of philosophical opinion on roughly the same matter and they both insist that it is a positive value. Is it that the pluralist takes the diversity to be terminal whereas the perennialist takes it to be only a kind of disguise? Perhaps. But then one must justify the diversity in some way that does not imply that it covers a fundamental unity. The temptation would be to regard various philosophical theories as interesting reactions to reality which reveal to us something of the individual philosopher and his times, etc. Now if this were taken as a criterion for appreciating philosophical diversity, at least two things must be said of it. One, it would infuriate, were they present, most objects of such appreciation: philosophers would by and large prefer to be found guilty of falsity than have their claim to our attention rest on their being "interesting." Second, such appreciation surely suggests a notion of the importance of philosophical diversity which provides community within that diversity. On a more basic level, moreover, one could suggest that pluralism is one view of the history of philosophy and that, on a thoroughgoing interpretation of pluralism, it is involved in an embarrassing paradox. For it seemingly must allow as equally justifiable a view of the history of philosophy which is the contradictory of pluralism.

To that last charge it could be replied that pluralism is not a philosophical view, but a meta-philosophical one. In reacting to that, I would invoke Aristotle's remark in the *Protrepticus*, quoted much earlier. Some of the criteria of meta-philosophy must belong to philosophy itself and, I should think, no meta-philosopher, no one who entertains views about philosophy's history and diversity, is really content to consider that diversity as terminal. (But again this is not the same as considering it terminable.) The conclusion would seem to be that any philosopher with an explicit view on philosophical diversity appeals to criteria which enable him to comment on that diversity and to that degree at least the diversity is not regarded as an ultimate unanalyzable fact. Needless to say, even the opinion that all or most of past philosophy has been radically mistaken and is thus ignorable counts as a view on philosophical diversity.

We have arrived at a point where we have in effect denatured the concept of perennial philosophy as many of its proponents want to employ it. For it is intended to be not just any view of the unity of the history of philosophy but a rather determinate view. We must inquire further, consequently, but as we do it will become apparent that there is a good deal of diversity as to the meaning of *philosophia perennis*.

There is a view of the perennial philosophy which would have it that one of the "systems" of philosophy actually embodies all the truths which have been discovered by man.

Scholastic philosophy, or, more restrictively, Thomism, is often urged as a candidate for this role. There is some ambiguity in the claim, particularly if the philosophy in question is considered to have reached its essential achievement and perfection centuries ago. A more modest way of making the claim consists of saying that whatever truths men discover will cohere and their coherence is possible because of certain basic principles, of reality, of thought, of a malevolent demon. Thus the philosophy which actually proceeds from principles that permit a constant assimilation of whatever truth arrives from whatever source could be considered the vehicle of the perennial philosophy. Of course the perennial philosophy so understood is something in process of revealing itself and the process would doubtless have to be considered unending. That corollary calls into question the possibility of regarding perennial philosophy as a system. Systematic, yes, since it is predicated on the unity and coherence of truths; a system, no, at least if a system is taken to be a self-enclosed whole, having a beginning, middle, and end.

Another view of the perennial philosophy does not assume that the plurality of philosophies can in some way be reduced to one of their number. Rather, it is the interplay of the various philosophies considered as autonomous which constitutes the perennial philosophy. Different philosophical systems, no matter how seemingly contradictory, are regarded as complementary, each but a partial view of a reality which can never be exhausted by the human mind and which is not therefore something accessible by means of one method or approach to the exclusion of others. On this view, the perennial philosophy is not a body of truths recognized willy-nilly by philosophers over the years, arrived at in spite as much as because of a particular method. Rather, it is a collection of half-truths each of which hint at some facet of the really real. All the hints are valuable; none takes absolute precedence over the others. In this understanding of perennial philosophy, it can be seen that truth in any strong sense of the term recedes into the background and is likely to be replaced by terms like suggestive, adequate, valuable, and relevant.

The great danger of the notion of a perennial philosophy, as Professor James Collins had pointed out,[18] is that it tends to regard the persistence, pervasiveness, and repetition of certain views, methods, and opinions as sufficient warrant of their philosophical importance, where this importance is read as a positive value. He rightly points out that many errors show persistence and crop up again and again in the history of philosophy. Now to make that observation requires, to be sure, a conception of philosophical truth and falsity which may appear to be the tenet of one school as opposed to others. Collins does not want simply to make this assumption; he argues that it must be made. Perhaps we can put his point in our own words and rejoin him to endorse his restricted theory of perennial philosophy.

The reader will recall that we got into the present discussion because we undertook to analyze the way in which other men can be of aid to us in our search for knowledge. The appeal to perennial philosophy is an appeal to an element in the *learning* of philosophy. Now, with respect to learning in the strong sense, we wanted to say that this process cannot be understood as coming to know what another thinks just as such, as terminal. There are criteria to which we must ultimately appeal in our assessment of what another says, criteria which are not themselves learned from others. If the perennial philosophy is spoken of as a catalogue of similar statements made by philosophers over the centuries, a listing of persistent attitudes, common assertions, similar methods, the compilation has as its effect to put us in possession of information about what others have said. To possess this information is not yet to have learned anything in the strong sense; the criterion for inclusion in the perennial philosophy is repetition or pervasiveness. The criterion for learning in the strong sense is found in the things spoken about, something we gain independently of what others have said and independently of what we may already have learned in the strong sense. There is no doubt that we will pay special attention to any opinion that is commonly held, particularly if it was held in quite different historical periods and by men who are otherwise at odds with one another. Aristotle, in sifting the opinions of his predecessors, always took such common agreements as a sign that the opinion could be true. But to judge that it is true, it is not sufficient simply to say that many or even all men hold it. Rather, we judge its truth by consulting what the statement is about.

Any notion of perennial philosophy which would withdraw completely from that kind of judgment can hardly be regarded as a philosophical view. One is tempted to think of it as a sociology of knowledge or as history in some limited sense—but I confess I am unclear on the precise nature of that temptation. It would not be knowledge in the strong sense, the sense that controls philosophy as we speak of it here; philosophical knowledge is not knowledge of what men say simply as what they say. And no matter how intricate and symmetrical a pattern could be detected in the views and opinions of men, insofar as those views and opinions purport to be about something other than our tendency to talk, it is what those views are about that provides the criteria for assessing them. This is why any philosophical conception of the perennial philosophy cannot regard the formal mediation between "systems" and methods as more than a preparation for philosophical judgment. No more could a philosophical conception of perennial philosophy involve the reduction of other systems of thought to a privileged system whose principles and methods are regarded as arbitrary or merely chosen.

The point just made would seem to be that insisted upon by Professor Collins. "At some point in one's defense of a perennial philosophy, one must make a direct examination of man's relation to being. What may be called an *extraperennialist* discussion about the nature of the real and of our knowledge of it is unavoidable when the question of philosophical truth is at stake."[19] Now this implies, among other things, that one must do philosophy before he can undertake assessments of philosophies and that, insofar as his assessment of philosophies may include, as a moment, the listing of common tenets, methods, problems, and so forth, as a philosophical enterprise it must eventually be brought to the point where judgments susceptible of truth are made. "Acknowledgment of being and its principles unites our philosophical judgments, not after the fashion of the perennialist orchestration, but through a common recognition of the same grounds of evidence and resolution for all our inferences."[20] Collins' conclusion is not that the notion of perennial philosophy has no worth but that it does not provide us with a criterion and ultimate determinant of philosophical truth. The worth of the notion of a perennial philosophy, he wants to say, is methodological and instrumental; it is something that keeps us open and receptive to the factual pluralism in philosophy. This openness to philosophical diversity is not a tendency toward eclecticism, toward a pastiche of positions gleaned from hither and yon which functions as a map of the historical terrain. The factual pluralism exhibited in the history of philosophy may be instructive in many ways; it may in many ways correct and alter our own views, but, philo-sophically considered, the instruction, correction, and altera-tion in question come about by an appeal to what the various views are views of. In short, what Collins derives from his study of the notion of perennial philosophy is an occasion for commending the role of knowledge of its history in our learning of philosophy. Before turning to that role, I want to say something of the importance of the foregoing for the situation that prompted this essay.

Catholics who profess embarrassment at the role assigned to Thomism in our intellectual life seem often to be appeal-ing to quite extra-philosophical criteria in calling it into ques-tion. One reads impatient articles whose burden is that no one today is in the least interested in the questions that en-gaged the scholastics; we are directed to the significance of certain cultural directions of the day, to the discussions which actually occupy philosophers and are urged to go and do likewise. Now it may very well be that the questions which interest contemporary philosophers are of philosophical mo-ment, but this is not something which can be grasped simply by observing the prevalence of the questions. It may very well be that many tenets of contemporary philosophers pos-sess authentic philosophical value, but this is not decided by observing how many hold them. It is unfortunate if philos-ophers have to be urged to occupy themselves with genuine philosophical contributions, but it would be a good deal less fortunate if our attitude toward philosophical activity were governed by wholly extra-philosophical criteria. It is not sim-ply a matter of going where the action is, of taking on the coloration of a present philosophical majority or of ingratiat-ing ourselves at all costs with those who hold dominating views. We can assume that the most sincere apostolic motives generate the kind of appeal to which I refer, for aren't we urged to make revealed truth appealing and relevant by employing the philosophy or philosophies currently in style? But before a philosopher can "employ" a philosophy he must make an assessment of it; he will want to know if it is truly worth bothering about. Moreover, a philosophical approach may be extremely worth-while for accomplishing the limited task for which it has been devised and be utterly worthless for the apologetic and theological role one might wish it to assume. What I am warning against is a muddle-headed pursuit of philosophies as fads, as contingent expressions of the day which the Catholic can employ to proportion the faith to his contemporaries' predilections. In the first place, not every philosophy will be flattered by this kind of attention and surely this is relevant to the efforts of those whose watchword is relevance. To state the obvious in the simplest terms, it is not prevalence or consensus or a quorum of the current arbiters of philosophical taste which determines whether a philosophical tenet or method has philosophical relevance. What if it should turn out that a current philosophical style is downright inimical to revealed truth? Surely one would be guilty of something more than social gaucherie if he seized upon such a philosophical method as an instrument of the Good News.

These rather obvious caveats will not be read by the serious-minded as an invitation to obscurantism. Professional philosophers should not be in need of extrinsic reminders, however woolly, to see that they have doubtless much to gain from paying attention to a philosophical current that has captured the fancy of many. They will assume, until the contrary be proven, if it ever is, that the prevalence of a philosophical attitude is a sign of its philosophical importance. But, being serious, they will try not to identify the recognition of the sign with a specifically philosophical judgment. Fur-

thermore, if they are Catholics, the importance of a philosophical view beyond the confines of mere philosophy will
not escape them. Given their different criteria of assessment,
philosophers cannot be expected to be unduly rattled by the
passing unpopularity of philosophical truths to which they
have won through with some difficulty; their more strident
advisers seem to be first over the rail whenever "Abandon
ship!" is heard. Just as consensus is not as such the mark of
philosophical truth, so unpopularity is not the conviction of
error. The philosopher comes to appreciate the deep truth of
the melancholy and oft-repeated observation that philosophical positions are not refuted but only abandoned. Aban-
donment here is a species of ignoring and that, however
poignant, cannot be construed as even a sign of the falsity
of a doctrine that has fallen from favor. Consider the following statement of that old truth. "No great philosophy has
ever been 'refuted.' It has rather been discarded as irrelevant,
irrelevant to another newly emerged type of intellectual and
cultural experience. The system of Aristotle was not refuted
by the gospels of the Hellenistic schools that followed after
it in time. Rather, the need for deliverance, for a way of salvation, grew more pressing than the Aristotelian desire to
understand. The imposing medieval syntheses, Arabic, Jewish, or Christian, were never refuted by the scientific human-
itarianisms to which men in search of emancipation turned.
Rather, men came to feel other values more insistent than
the intellectual and spiritual values they had enabled men to
secure. And if the scientific and humanistic philosophies of
our own time are destined to be superseded by other and more
dogmatic views of nature and human society, it will not be
because they have been 'disproved.'"[21] This suite of philosophical attitudes suggests that the controlling factors of the
alterations within the history of philosophy are not always

philosophical, that the assessment of philosophical relevance is often unphilosophical. Were this only partially true, it would indicate why those in search of knowledge about man and circumambient reality consult the history of philosophy with the expectation that among "superseded" doctrines they may find both positive and negative aid for arriving at philosophical truth. Collins had made the point already in speaking of one of the functions of perennial philosophy conceived as a method rather than as a body of doctrine. One might come to see that philosophical diversity is not always grounded in philosophical causes, that is, is dictated not by the way things are but by factors which may be broadly cultural or narrowly subjective and idiosyncratic. This of course raises severe questions regarding progress in philosophy. Critics like Adler and Reichenbach[22] are saying something different from this when they maintain that philosophy's past has been checkered and confused: they are passing a philosophical judgment on past positions which they render quite present and competing in the process. In any case, one who would learn philosophy cannot be disinterested in its history on the easy assumption that the old is forgotten and rightly so because it has been surpassed. Age finally counts neither for nor against a philosophical doctrine; at least in many of its disciplines, philosophy is in search of truths which are not a function of an historical period or contingent outlook. If such truths there be, they will be at once timely and timeless. Perhaps the truths regarded as least relevant in a given historical epoch are precisely those of which it stands most in need. Were that ever true those whose concern is the good of men living in a particular time would be well advised not to take the word of their contemporaries as to what is relevant and what is irrelevant.

Tradition and the Individual Talent

I borrow here with some sense of the impropriety of doing so the title of an essay by T. S. Eliot. In that essay, Eliot speaks of poetic creativity and its relation to the whole tradition of poetry and what he has to say seems to me important, *mutatis mutandis*, for the study of philosophy. First, to get it out in the open, I want to invoke a terse comment in Eliot's essay. Someone objects that the old writers are less interesting to us because we know so much more than they did. Precisely, Eliot replies, and they are that which we know. The image Eliot creates is of poetry as a living whole, beginning with Homer and extending to the present. The poet who has a truly original voice is judged to have it in terms of the tradition to which he adds and which he subtly alters by adding to it. Now I am not of course concerned here with Eliot's views on tradition and creativity in poetry, but what I want to say has been influenced by his essay which, incidentally, I first read long before I began the study of philosophy.

In speaking earlier of learning philosophy, we stressed the fact that the novice brings to his listening criteria which enable him to assess what he hears. But of course it is most often the case that the one who teaches us philosophy is concerned to bring to our attention a vast amount of philosophical literature and the voice we hear is not simply his; rather a chorus of great minds addresses us and a kind of piety (or intimidation) is produced which postpones the critical appraisal which learning requires. When one acquires some sensitivity to the reverence in which Plato and Aristotle have been held over the centuries, he may feel less than eager to pass judgment on what they have said. Moreover, he comes to see that what they had said is by no means easily accessible to a twentieth-century reader. There is the language, of course; even if he has studied Greek, the instruction probably has not taken to the point where he feels perfectly at home with the original text. And there are countless difficulties with the text itself. It, too, has a history and one gets into the position of having to trust not only translators but the editors of the text that has been translated. Beyond this more or less material level, there is the question of the Greek outlook on man and nature and God and knowledge, an outlook which, even if one eventually comes to hold that it contains persistent and common elements, has as well features which are contingent and explicable only in terms of an historical epoch. How is one to react to all these considerations? He might turn away in despair. He might proceed with cavalier insouciance to pass swift judgments in the absence of true historical understanding. Or he may decide to take the painful route which leads him circuitously to the point where he can make a responsible philosophical use of what Plato said. Meanwhile, time has passed and one is scarcely into Plato. Again despair beckons. But if one turns from the ancients before making a philosophical appraisal of them, what assurance does he have that there is a short cut to what he seeks? Contemporary philosophers may be more accessible on many counts, but most of them have a way of speaking of their predecessors and one will be in no position to pass even an historical, let alone a philosophical, judgment on those *obiter dicta*. No matter, perhaps; they speak substantively as well. But if difficulties of language and text diminish when we turn to our contemporaries, the other difficulties made up of unquestioned assumptions and vagrant interests are aggravated for we may share the assumptions unwittingly and be even less capable of criticizing them. The individual talent seems thus to be swallowed up by tradition, whether tradition is regarded as extending into ancient times or made up only of what our contemporaries are saying. For there are a great many contemporary philosophers. Reichenbach held that philosophy really began with Kant, and we might feel grateful for the restriction; but even if philosophy were considered to have begun in 1900, the task of catching up would be enormous. When, the numbed novice may inquire, when will the possibility of making any contribution to philosophy arise? When learning philosophy is seen in terms of tradition, and there is no other way of seeing it however foreshortened the tradition be, it seems an endless pursuit where almost no one will be able to make a significant contribution since the vast majority of us grow old reading furiously.

The simple fact of the matter is that few of us are destined to say anything which will mark a genuine advance in philosophy. The simple fact of the matter is that "new philosophies" more often than not are not new with any conscious and sustained comparison with what is old. Nothing is more depressing than checking out references to past philosophy in a given thinker. Thus Wittgenstein begins his *Philosophical Investigations* by referring to a remark of Augustine's on learning language. The citation is to the *Confessions*, and one has to wonder if Wittgenstein was aware of the *De magistro*. But Wittgenstein was not interested in doing the history of philosophy, we will be told; he was interested in clearing up confusions. Whose confusions? The confusions of philosophers, as it happens, among whom Augustine chances to be numbered. His own confusions, too, certainly, but whence did these arise and mightn't they have been avoided by consulting his philosophical elders? Which is more impertinent, that suggestion or Wittgenstein's practice?

What I am getting at is this: our criteria for philosophical novelty can easily become hazy. Men have been in search of knowledge for a long time, and this search has been productive of a tradition, rather of traditions, and when one takes these traditions seriously into account, when he takes any one of them seriously into account, any early ambitions he might have had of contributing to the philosophical enterprise can come to seem a matter of youthful juiciness, for there is a long road to go before it is clear to him that what he has to say is indeed a contribution. Despite the difficulties involved in the appropriation of a tradition, moreover, they are small indeed when compared with those which would attend starting from scratch.

What is wrong with the foregoing is that it seems to suggest that in order to learn anything we must consult everything that has been said or written on the matter which interests us. But that is patently absurd. If someone wishes to speak about language, for instance, we can compare what he has to say with our own experience of what he is talking about. In doing so, we make an assessment. True, it may be a tentative judgment, particularly if we are inclined to think that the speaker has more in mind than comes through to us immediately. But say we become convinced of the accuracy of what he says. If we do, we are no longer dependent in our judgment on the fact that he said it. Now the knowledge we thereby gain is new to us, but we are in no position to say that what we have learned is a new view of language (even if the speaker assures us it is, with many or few references to his predecessors). That is, we are in no position to say that a view of a contemporary philosopher is a new view simply on his say-so or by consulting the copyright. Once more, a small point, but it can be important, for if we make that unwarranted assumption we may acquire the conviction that we would have nothing to gain by consulting the predecessors of our informant. This indifference to past philosophy, based on the assumption that recent philosophy is both new and adequate, is fairly widespread among certain philosophers today. But does it really make any difference?

It is not only possible but likely that nowadays a student is introduced to philosophy by being told that a revolution has taken place in the field. He doesn't yet know what philosophy is but he is assured that it is now quite different from what it used to be. From his teachers he acquires an attitude of condescension toward whole centuries of intellectual effort: Kant whom he has not read he is disposed to regard as quaint, Descartes as curious, Leibnitz as ludicrous, Hegel as hilarious, and the Scholastics as—scholastic. These poor devils had the misfortune to be born prior to the twentieth century when, it is well known, a revolution took place in philosophy. Furthermore, and here the irony becomes delicious, this condescending attitude is said to be a consequence of a more modest view of the philosophical task. A cavalier dismissal of centuries of honest intellectual effort parades as modesty! Men who have cupped Western philosophy momentarily in their palm and then cast it disdainfully away characterize themselves as eschewing a comprehensive view! They in their modesty are content with small questions, limited tasks, piecemeal work. History is bunk, said Henry Ford. On the philosophical scene there are those who have an equally charming faith in the value of the latest model. But is philosophy at all comparable to industrial progress? Have we indeed surpassed previous inquiries into the ultimate questions: What is man? What is his destiny? How does he differ from other things under the sun? What should he do? These are questions the seriousness of which most men need no help in recognizing; these are questions that men bring to philosophy and philosophy, by which we mean human intellectual inquiry in all its natural scope, must address itself to these questions. Surely there is something phony about a philosophical revolution which has as its result the putting away of those questions, the assertion that it is not up to the philosopher to answer them, which has as its goal not the handling of these questions but their suppression. One is reminded of Kierkegaard's remark about Cratylus' advance on Heraclitus, thanks to which the basic tenet of Heraclitus was rendered meaningless. Poor Heraclitus, to have such a disciple, Kierkegaard said. So one can regard the "revolution in philosophy" and say, Poor philosophy.

Whether in learning philosophy we turn to past or present philosophers and thereby involve ourselves in a long or truncated tradition, the net effect may seem to be a postponing of any attempt to answer the questions that brought us to philosophy in the first place. For we may easily get bogged down in history and philology; we may find ourselves becoming expert in the writings of one man or one school, whether ancient, medieval, or modern, and a tendency to footnote rather than to argue is felt. If we begin with older authors, we may on occasion justify our specialty by saying there is nothing new under the philosophical sun; if we begin with our contemporaries, we may regard philosophy on an analogy with plumbing or technology and take it as given that the twentieth century represents an unquestioned advance over its predecessors. When we speak of the past, it will be with the cloacal humor of a Chick Sales talking of outdoor facilities. To learn philosophy by applying for instruction to authors or teachers is to become involved in a tradition; to accept what is handed down, and to become involved in a tradition has disadvantages we have not even begun to explore. When dissatisfaction sets in, as inevitably it will if we are at all intellectually alive, we may continue to philosophize but do so against a background of rejection of all we have hitherto read or heard. But this is but another way to relate to a tradition; one continues to make covert or overt reference to one's unhappy philosophical youth. And ironically, one may, like Descartes, carry over from the rejected tradition a host of sophisticated tenets now regarded as commonplace truths. The odd thing is that we must already be involved in a philosophical tradition in order to react to it and even if our reaction seems wholly negative what we then proceed to do has much of its significance with reference to the rejected tradition. In short, the individual talent in philosophy can manifest itself, can be appraised, only in the light of tradition. For most of us the most we can hope to do is to make our own what our predecessors and preceptors have known. This is a recognition that will depress us only if we import into philosophy a concept of originality which is appropriate to other human activities. The originals in philosophy are a small elite; the idiosyncratics are legion. What ultimately counts, of course, is not that a teaching is new, not that it is mine, but rather that, in the appropriate sense, it is true. This recognition calls for a self-effacement of which few of us are capable and it is that lack of self-effacement which is partly responsible for the factual pluralism in philosophy. In short, and this is a point we would all like to avoid, the individual talent must be guided by appropriate moral attitudes. But that is something to which we shall turn later.

Summary

This essay is addressed to those who, like its author, are Catholics concerned about the present state of the philosophy engaged in by Catholics. This concern arises out of a decisive historical phenomenon of our own day, namely, Vatican II which stemmed from Pope John's call for an *aggiornamento*. When one looks over the past fifty years or so of Catholic philosophy in America, what greets his eye is not likely to produce unbounded elation. The philosophy taught in our colleges and seminaries bills itself as Thomistic and it is an institutional response to the call of an earlier pope, Leo XIII, for an intellectual renewal in the Church. The response may seem to leave just about everything to be desired. With exceptions notable almost because of their rarity as because of their substantive contributions, Catholics have not been doing well philosophically and they have been out of contact with their contemporaries. Moreover, contemporary philosophy gives the impression of excitement and progress and debate and these are not precisely the marks of the philosophy that has become official with Catholics. How easy then to attribute our difficulties to the suffocating effects of tradition, how understandable to suggest that we shake ourselves loose from tradition and enter the market place of ideas and follow the going arguments whither they might lead. The feeling is current that there is something unique about philosophy as it is engaged in by Catholics and that one characteristic of that uniqueness, questions of simple talent aside, is precisely deference to tradition. Now admittedly there is an initial plausibility in this reaction. However, and this has been the purpose of the chapter we are now bringing to a close, when we begin to reflect on learning philosophy, abstracting from whether or not the learner is a Catholic, it seems to be fairly clear that anyone who learns philosophy, in the sense we have assigned the phrase, is involved in what can only be called a tradition. To learn from another is to accept what is handed down by another. Involvement in a tradition, accordingly, is not peculiar to one way of learning philosophy; it is part and parcel of what is meant by learning philosophy.

That is our first point and there is no need to consult a seismograph to assess its impact; it is almost trivially obvious. But isn't it sometimes overlooked in impatient polemics? Given our first point, we are forced to consider different ways of being involved in a tradition and it is here the notion of authority rears its head. If we say that learning is the process whereby we heed what another is handing on to us, we must admit that the possibility exists of someone stopping right there. One might fill his head, or notebook, with what another says, with what another has written. This is the question he asked; here is his answer. Our second point was that this kind of involvement in tradition, far from being a necessary result of learning, is actually a short-circuiting of it, a failure to benefit from tradition. When we learn from another we first attend to the question he asks, the problem he works up; if his question is not ours, if his problem does not engage us, something is wrong already. Either one is not listening in the appropriate way or he is unlucky in his teacher. If the teacher is deserving of the name and if one is listening as he ought so that the question becomes truly a question for him, one for which there seem to be a number of possible answers, he can heed the answer posed by his teacher. The culmination and point of the process is the assessment of the answer. To what criteria does the learner appeal in order to make this assessment, in order to learn? He appeals to what the teacher is speaking of, that out of which the question arose, an area of experience accessible to him apart from any ministrations and aid from anybody else. Surely the one thing we cannot learn from another is experience of the area under discussion. Truly to learn, then, is to acquire a truth about an area of reality, and a sign that this has been accomplished is that reference to the person of the teacher or to the learner as possessing the truth is an unnecessary addendum. It is no longer a matter of what *he* thinks or of what *I* think but of the way things are. There may be all kinds of gradations in learning, gradations explainable as much as anything by the things in question, but whatever can be learned is ultimately detachable from biography and autobiography. And that, as we have suggested, has its ramifications for any discussion of tradition and the individual talent.

Having argued for the inevitability of tradition and having emphasized that some objections to the effect of tradition are objections to its failure rather than to its successes, we then explored advantages and disadvantages of tradition. It is perhaps easier to perceive the leaden echo. To get involved in what men have had to say, whether these men are separated from us in time or our contemporaries, may entail either a tremendous amount of erudition, a lengthy attention to the instruments of learning, and these can easily turn into impediments, or it can conduce to an insouciant and mindless dismissal of the past in favor of the latest word, something which can have as its effect the consolidation of our unquestioned prejudices and myths. To turn to the past may be to set out on a journey from which no traveler returns; to opt for the present may be to cut oneself off from documents which would facilitate gaining answers to good and perennial questions.

It is the hope that, despite the wrangling among them, philosophers may have succeeded over the years in coming up with some solid answers to pervasive questions, that underlies the notion of a perennial philosophy. We discussed this notion in its employment as a device to get above the shocking diversity among philosophers and saw that a great danger in it is that it can turn out to be an extra-philosophical assessment of philosophical doctrines. That is, if criteria for the ingredients of the perennial philosophy are repetition, pervasiveness, and longevity, there will be many items in the perennial philosophy which are false, since some falsehoods exhibit all these characteristics. If it is objected that such an importation of truth and falsity is inappropriate since it amounts to appealing to one school's notion of what is true and what is false, the objection exhibits the danger in perennial philosophy we pointed to. Is the alternative to select one philosophy as the perennial philosophy and to regard the others as unfortunate divergences from the straight and narrow path? Our suggestion was that the alternative is to get off this meta-philosophical plane, not only because no one can begin there, but because it defeats the purpose of doing philosophy. That purpose we want now to recall and thereby end our summary.

To philosophize is to adjust cognitively to the world in which we are. That is, to be a man in a full sense is to wonder about the situation in which we find ourselves. Quite spontaneously, one wonders what he as opposed to other cosmic things is; one wonders about his own destiny and what he should do; one wonders about the cosmos, too, its whence and what and whither. Just as one speaks prose before being aware he is doing so, so most men ask the questions which make up philosophy or can easily be induced to ask them, *ceteris paribus*. Philosophy, as we are using the term, is simply a more formal and conscious addressing of ourselves to those questions. The questions arise out of our experience of reality and it is reality to which appeal must finally be made in order to assess answers to them. Finally it makes little difference whether the answers are old or new, perennial or not. The single value we wanted to get out of the notion of perennial philosophy, and this at the suggestion of Collins, is that it keeps us sensitive to the fact that teachers other than our present ones, authors other than those we currently read, have things to say which will increase our grasp of the way things are. The true import of the notion of perennial philosophy is not its seemingly subjective reference, its calling of our attention to the variety of philosophers and philosophies, but rather its objective reference, its pointing to a various and never perfectly plumbed reality.

NOTES

1. There is an extensive literature on the relation between myth and philosophy. *See* my *A History of Western Philosophy, Vol. 1, Beginnings to Plotinus*, Chicago, 1963. See also Gary Wills, *Chesterton, Man and Mask*, New York, 1961, pp. 186–90 for interesting remarks on Chesterton's views on myth as expressed in *The Everlasting Man*.

2. G. E. Moore once said that he doubted he would have had any philosophical problems apart from reading philosophers. This is a wry remark, I think, and could be read as a strong statement of the view suggested in the text. Later I will suggest that philosophizing does not begin with the reading of philosophers.

3. See Aquinas, *Quaestio disputata de veritate*, q. 11, a. 1.

4. Kant gives these questions in *Kritik der Reinen Vernunft*. B 832 ff. Cf. Martin Heidegger, *Kant und das Problem der Metaphysik*, Frankfurt, 1951, pp. 185 ff.

5. Josef Pieper, "The Concept of Tradition," *The Review of Politics*, Vol. 20, No. 4, pp. 465–91.

6. Mortimer Adler, *The Conditions of Philosophy*, New York, 1965.

7. S. Toulmin in *Metaphysical Beliefs*, London, 1957.

8. See Sidney Hook's essay, "Scientific Knowledge and Philosophical Knowledge" in his *The Quest for Being*, New York, 1961.

9. See below, Chapter Four, the discussion of chatter and jargon.

10. N. R. Hanson, *Patterns of Discovery*, Cambridge, 1961; David Schon, *Displacement of Concepts*, London, 1963; B. Lonergan, S.J., *Insight*, London, 1957.

11. M. Polanyi, *Science, Faith and Society*, Chicago, 1964.

12. The notion of the starting point of philosophy is an ambiguous one. My point here is that, while an ideal or achieved starting point is a legitimate sense of the phrase, the achieved must be put into relation with the given and if the given is messy that fact may be a message. From where do we set out to achieve the ideal starting point? The answer to that question, far from being irrelevant to talk of the achieved starting point, is essential to it.

13. Jean-François Revel, *Pourquoi des philosophes?* Paris, 1957. The notion that philosophy is destined to disappear with the advance of science is strong in Comte and positivism generally and repeated by J. L. Austin. See his discussion of his paper, "Performative/Constative" in Charles E. Caton, *Philosophy and Ordinary Language*, Urbana, Illinois, 1963, p. 42.

14. See M. Evans Monroe, *The Language of Mathematics*, Ann Arbor, 1963.

15. See Sir David Ross, *Aristotle's De Anima*, edited with an introduction and commentary, Oxford, 1961, p. 17.

16. Karl Jaspers may be a kind of exception; however, although he regards philosophical documents as more or less equally ciphers of transcending, he is not open to the claim that they can be anything more. See Jeanne Hersch, "Is Jaspers Conception of Tradition Adequate for Our Times?" and James Collins, "Jaspers on Science and Philosophy" in *The Philosophy of Karl Jaspers*, ed. P. Schilpp, New York, 1957.

17. See P. Gleason, "Pluralism and the New Pluralism," *America*, Vol. CX, March 7, 1964, pp. 308–12.

18. James Collins, "The Problem of a Perennial Philosophy," in *Three Paths in Philosophy*, Chicago, 1962, pp. 255–79.

19. *Ibid.*, p. 271.

20. *Ibid.*, p. 274.

21. J. H. Randall, Jr., *How Philosophy Uses Its Past*, New York, 1963, p. 21.

22. H. Reichenbach, *The Rise of Scientific Philosophy*, Berkeley, 1951.

CHAPTER THREE

PHILOSOPHY AND FAITH

The question of the effects of faith on philosophy can be raised in close continuity with our discussion of the notion of tradition. In the foregoing chapter, having pointed out that whoever learns philosophy is by that very fact involved in a tradition, we went on to speak of a variety of ways of being so involved. We even indulged ourselves to the extent of speaking of opting for a contemporary tradition as opposed to an older one. It is important that we see now how misleading and unreal such talk of opting is.

"Come on in, the water's fine," would be an absurd invitation coming from someone standing fully clothed and with undamp hair at poolside. It would be equally absurd to expect that anyone would have views on tradition's impact on philosophy before having engaged in the study of philosophy. The whole thing has to be retrospective; it has to issue from someone already in the swim of things. Our present question can be put this way, "Did he jump or was he pushed?"

The Catholic who finds that simply in virtue of the fact that he has gone to a given school he has been introduced to a certain kind of philosophy, one perhaps that derives from St. Thomas Aquinas, may feel indignant about not having been consulted beforehand. On a matter of such moment, he may come to feel, he should have been presented with the alternatives and permitted to choose. As it is, he has already put in several semesters, let us say, and he can never regain the philosophical innocence that was his before he took any courses. In his disenchantment—let us imagine someone who is unhappy with what he has contacted in his philosophy courses—he may conjure up an ideal situation in which, before one commences the study of philosophy, he passes in review the various ways of beginning and in the end makes a reasonable choice. True, one could come to regret a choice so made, but at least the regret would be for one's own mistake and not that of an institution. Before exploring the possibility of such a choice, let us consider a number of other ways in which one might get involved in philosophy other than the way our disgruntled Catholic did.

To begin with the trivial and capricious, we might imagine someone taking shelter from the rain in a bookstore and finding himself in the section labeled "Philosophy and Phrenology." Bored and mildly curious, he permits his eye to graze along the shelves until his fancy is caught by a handsomely bound volume, its leather glinting in the half-light of the shop. He removes it from the shelf, he admires its heft in his hand, the supple almost sensuous rippling of the cover. Opening it, he lets its spine rest in his palm and pages with growing interest through it. After a moment he begins to read. "It was Descartes," he says afterward. "The *Discourse on Method*. It changed my life." A committed Cartesian, in other words, and that is just what we want. Now, if we should ask him why he began the study of philosophy with Descartes—a serious fellow, his library now consists largely of the philosophers—he may be tempted to say that Descartes is the natural starting point. Or, given Descartes' reputation, what better place? But he is honest and would doubtless admit that he began with Descartes because he knew enough to come in out of the rain, because the copy of Descartes appealed to his bibliophilic and aesthetic sense. He just *happened* to start with Descartes. It could as easily have been

Denis the Areopagite, Swedenborg, Schelling, or Lucretius. He might want to say that if he had indeed picked up one of those it is unlikely he would ever have become interested in philosophy. But that would prove only that attraction to and flight from philosophy could equally be due to chance.

Another imaginary situation. Sidney enrolls at Neurotic State, signs up for a course in animal husbandry, and, thanks to an errant IBM card, finds himself in Philosophy I. Five minutes into the first class meeting he suspects the horrible truth and, turning to Krishna, the pneumatic blonde beside him, starts to ask if this is animal husbandry. Smitten by her beauty, Sidney's mouth moves but words do not emerge. No matter. He would stay now if the class were advanced metaphysics. The weeks pass, Sidney's ardor for Krishna cools, his defense drops and he finds himself following the lecture. He is fascinated. *Et cetera.* Years later, Sidney, now Associate Professor of Philosophy at Tic Tech, finds himself a member of a self-study committee financed by the Sand Foundation. In the course of an extempore homily on the need for a more rational sequence in the philosophy offerings, he is beset by memories of IBM cards, of animal husbandry, of Krishna. He falls silent. What troubles him? The *lacrimae rerum,* a consuming sense of *temps perdu?* Perhaps. But there is an outside chance he is thinking of the utter irrationality of the circumstances that attended his own induction into the ranks of the philosophers. Like the man who came in out of the rain, Sidney can blame (or praise) no institutional program for his beginning; Sidney can only point to what Nathanael West called the Chauffeur within.

If we move on to more reasonable beginnings, we could consider a young man whose Uncle George, whom he respects highly, urges him to read the *Critique of Pure Reason.*

"No boy should be without a copy," Uncle George says at first and, later, "Without a thorough grounding in the *Critique* no one can be considered an educated man." Now this is pretty heady talk for the nephew and we are not surprised to see him sprinting off to the library. If we should ask him after the lapse of years why he began with Kant, he would say that he took Uncle George's advice. He trusted Uncle George. Now for Uncle George we can substitute, in the experience of most of us, a college adviser, a curriculum committee that made Philosophy I a required course, good old St. Philomena's College, or an article in *Time*. Most of us took somebody's word for the way we became introduced to philosophy and most of us were relatively unconscious that we were doing so. It is only in retrospect, perhaps, that we become aware that of various modes of entree we were directed to one.

The upshot of the foregoing, then, is this. There are two general ways of beginning the study of philosophy. One is by chance and the other is by following someone's advice. Now the disgruntled young Catholic we spoke of a moment ago may meaningfully contrast what happened to him with what happened to the boy in the bookstore on a rainy day or with what happened to Sidney. But how does his experience differ from that of the nephew who took his uncle's advice or of students in other colleges who were advised to take or had to take philosophy? It would seem that there is no significant difference, at least not of the kind he in his disenchantment imagined.

What he imagined, remember, was some way in which the various philosophies or the various ways to begin the study of philosophy were passed in review so that a choice could be made of one of them. So be it. Let the play be played. In terms of what would one who had not previously studied philosophy choose? For what does it mean to pass the possibilities in review? Surely not to study each philosophy in turn or to try out various modes of introduction, for then inevitably one would be in the water already. One might listen to descriptions of philosophies and of ways to begin, but what is being described is what others have done and what one might do. To put it more specifically, if the choice is being thought of under the general aegis of what is the best way to gain help from others in answering such questions as, Is death the end? What should I do? What can I know? What is knowledge? etc.—well, then, on that assumption, in order to make a choice, one must take someone's word for the value of this man or that, this method or that. Wouldn't it be strange if a young man, about to start the study of philosophy, should say to his adviser, "You're right!" How could he know the adviser is right before he has followed the advice?

If the foregoing is not without connection with the way things are, the kind of choice envisaged by our disgruntled novice would not transport him into a situation radically different from the one he is now lamenting. He may be angry with the advisers he has had but in the possibility he imagines the beginner would still be dependent on the advice of others or on the reputation of authors—but reputation is only a kind of anonymous advice.

The general conclusion I want to draw is this. Anyone who begins the study of philosophy, who undertakes to learn it in the sense of learning developed in the previous chapter, is put in the position of having to believe the route he is taking is a good one. He is trusting someone. This is only what we would expect, of course, since learning philosophy is a social affair and trust is the basis of society. Yet this is a truism it is well to recall at the present juncture when dissatisfaction with the way philosophy has been taught in Catholic colleges leads to implicit or explicit appeal to a way of beginning philosophy which is quite simply impossible of realization. It is not what everyone else does because it is what no one could do. The Catholic, then, is in this respect in a generic situation, not a unique one. This does not mean that criticism of his specific situation is impossible and that we should not consider ways in which students could more effectively be introduced to philosophy. But whatever plan we come up with, be it ever so flawless and exciting, it will remain something the fledgling in philosophy, the boy or girl arcing a mental toe for the first time toward the philosophical waters, will have to take our word for. Whether programs are old or new, good or bad, those who come under them have to trust their framers that they are effective and good.

I reserve for the moment a consideration of no small importance, namely, the advantage of the Catholic in this matter. If the Catholic, like everyone else, has to trust others when he commences the study of philosophy, recalling this may remove the embarrassment some apparently feel at the realization that from the very outset they were told what philosophy to study. It turns out that in some sense everyone is in the same boat. But there are boats and boats, trust and trust, advice and advice. For the Catholic, the ordinary magisterium of the Church will carry slightly more weight than an *obiter dictum* of Uncle George. What if that which embarrasses some Catholics is not only an instance of a universal situation but, within the universal situation, an infinitely preferable and more efficacious way of being introduced to philosophy?

Knowing and Believing

When one has made the point that at the outset of the study of philosophy, when we begin to learn philosophy, faith or trust in others is required, he must go on to insist that such faith is temporary and not terminal; we trust others because by following their advice we hope to arrive at a point where it will no longer be necessary to trust them in order to know: the believing at issue here is destined to be overcome by knowledge. Quite obviously, what we are now saying is simply another way of speaking of the proper way to benefit from a tradition. And just as one who becomes involved in a tradition has other resources than what is told him, so too the trust which is necessary if we are to learn is not something utterly blind and unquestioning. We may suspend disbelief on certain points but we can do this only because on other points we know. For example, when we are told to accept something rather obscure on the promise that it will later be clarified, we do so if we do because other connected matters are not unclear. There are a number of mental attitudes at play here and something may be gained by looking briefly at each.

We have contrasted in an initial way knowing and believing, but what we have said can be seen to involve such attitudes as supposing, thinking (in the sense of having an opinion), and doubting. If by knowing we mean a judgment whose warrant is a direct acquaintance with certain things, that judgment may be thought of as expressible in a proposition whose truth or falsity is decided by more or less direct reference to the things spoken of. Knowing would differ from opinion in this that the subject matter effectively closes inquiry in the case of knowledge but not in that of opinion. To think that such-and-such is the case, to have an opinion, may be based on acquaintance with a given subect matter when it is precisely the subject matter which prevents us from saying we know in the strong sense. What we hold is more likely than not the case, but it is possible, however remotely, that it is not the case.

Aquinas spoke of the opposition between knowing and opining in the following way.[1] Since the judgments involved are expressible in propositions, knowledge is such that the contradictory of what is known is unconditionally rejected because of the evidence one has. In the case of opinion, a proposition is accepted but with the recognition that its contradictory might be true. Inquiry, which can issue in knowledge or opinion, is thus thought of as addressing two contradictory propositions and asking which is true. To doubt a proposition is to suspect that its contradictory is more likely to be true; to suppose something is to treat a proposition as true for some purpose. Much more could be said of each of these, of course, but on the basis of the little that has been said it can be seen why one could not have knowledge and opinion of the same matter. This is not to say that an opinion is never spoken of as knowledge or that knowledge is never introduced as one's opinion. Nevertheless, it is possible to assign meanings to these terms, meanings which are not arbitrary and which in many respects accord with common usage, thanks to which knowledge and opinion can be definitively opposed. What now of faith?

The title of this chapter suggests an opposition between philosophy, what can be known and what can be opined, on the one hand, and, on the other, what is believed by religious faith. That is the opposition we are ultimately interested in, of course, but we are trying to approach it by way of a garden variety of faith, human faith, the trust one man can place in another. So soon as we put it this way we are reminded of the familiar tenet to the effect that to believe is at once to believe something and someone.[2] In speaking of the way in which we begin the formal study of philosophy (putting aside the purely adventitious ways of beginning, though this is not to say that chance may not enter into the choice of a school, etc.), we wanted to say that we believe someone about the best way to begin that study. The one we believe may be Uncle George, a counselor, a curriculum committee, or something far vaguer like the tradition of a school, and what we believe is that such and such a course, a certain author or authors, a given period in the history of philosophy, represents a good starting point for our study of philosophy. At the outset we can't know or even in any full sense have an opinion that what we accept is true. If we accept it we do so because someone has said it. Our conclusion is that it is an extremely common thing for people to begin the study of philosophy on the basis of trust in someone's word, that the judgment we make, a judgment exemplified in our following the advice, is made in terms of extra-philosophical criteria. For we do of course make a judgment, but what we appeal to is the credibility of our adviser, our feeling that he has no reason to mislead us, etc.

Once this common situation is recognized, it is possible to discuss the similarity and difference between the Catholic and non-Catholic in this area. The Catholic is given advice by the Church as to how he might best begin the study of philosophy and the Church, for the Catholic, is a good deal more trustworthy than any merely human agency. Thus, within the common situation, in this tricky area, the Catholic will be far better off than his non-Catholic fellows. The certitude he feels that he is beginning in the proper way is not based on the reputation of a random individual or committee or college. His response to the Church's advice is englobed by his belief that the Church is no merely human agency, that it has a providential role to play in the affairs of men, that even on matters outside its immediate and proper province, on matters like the study of philosophy, the Church's word can be accepted in a way that is qualitatively distinct from just any reliance on the word of another. Things are not unequivocally bright for the Catholic, however, since a great many things intervene between the advice of the Church, which is quite generic, and the curriculum at St. Philomena's. But before discussing that, there is a prior point that must be taken up. Does it really matter where we begin the study of philosophy?

If learning philosophy implies some kind of trust or faith at its outset, this is merely a moment in what we have called getting involved in a tradition, a moment which must be followed by a judgment in the light of the facts. That is, we have not really learned if we maintain something because someone has said it; rather we must subject what he says to the test of what he is talking about and what he is talking about must be accessible to us independently of what anyone says of it. The faith and trust we have been speaking of here are, accordingly, a vanishing item and the more quickly they vanish the better. If that is so, it does not seem to matter a great deal where we begin the study of philosophy because if we are seriously engaged in it, if we learn, we will be making judgments which cut the umbilical cord, so to speak, we will be making judgments which are autonomous and ours.

Ideally perhaps it would make no difference where we begin the study of philosophy, but it is well to spell out what that "ideally" implies. In the first place, it implies that we are quite unaffected by the authority and reputation of the author we are reading or of the professor we are hearing, but quite dispassionately and without deviation subject what he is saying to the test. Furthermore, it implies that we are quite incapable of being misled, that our mind unerringly goes to the truth of the matter. Finally, and this increases the unreality of the supposed situation, it implies that philosophers generally present what they have to say in a fashion that makes it easy for their readers or listeners to connect it with what is already known. This would demand that their language bears at least a family resemblance to the language of ordinary life, that their problems bear a like resemblance, and so forth. But the common experience of men calls this ideal situation into question. Far more than pure intellect is at play when we subject ourselves to philosophical instruction; we are influenced by non-rational factors not simply to get into the door of the classroom, or into a given author, but long afterward. It is well that we be tentative in passing judgments at the outset of our study; we have to get acclimated, after all, but in the process what we hear becomes familiar and takes on a kind of sanction from that familiarity which is not unlike the component of "common sense" we spoke of in the previous chapter.[3] And consider the philosophers with whom we might begin. We could be introduced to a jargon so unrelated to ordinary life and our pre-philosophical certitudes that it would never occur to us to try to relate the two; in short, rather than passing a judgment we would become indisposed to make judgments. Not only that, but there are many philosophers whose stock in trade consists of casting doubt on the total content of what we have called common sense, philosophers who call into doubt the reality of external objects, who call into doubt our ability to know anything whatsoever with certitude, philosophers who speak to packed halls of their incertitude as to whether they are really there. Of course no one takes this kind of problem seriously, least of all the philosopher who professes to have it. He may spend fifty minutes doubting the reality of the walls, but he always leaves the room by the door. The net effect of this is to induce a game-like attitude, to create the impression that philosophy is the enterprise in which we make believe, in which we utter preposterous things in a patently unserious way. There are instructors of philosophy, and everyone has met them, whose personal lives are a frightful mess but who have taken on with an almost messianic zeal the task of calling into question for undergraduates what they are pleased to call "bourgeois morality." The example, it seems to me, is crucial for the suggestion that it really does not matter where we begin the study of philosophy or with whom or with what or how. Consider the philosophical neophyte, an undergraduate at an age when passion is strong and reason easily clouded by emotion; place him in a class where moral values are called into question in a radical fashion, where temperance and chastity are archly discussed as fossils of surpassed emotive attitude toward human life. That what is maintained can be shown to be nonsense doesn't really matter. Our attention must be called to his audience, to the forces that would be at work within young people and which make the position maintained attractive. The morally corruptive effect of such an introduction to philosophy, while not inevitable, is hardly surprising. And, lest this caution seem inimical to the plea that the unexamined life is not worth living, remember that one of the principal targets of Socrates' scorn were teachers who corrupt the morals of the young under the guise of the search for truth.

The best and basic analogue for talk of education is the family, the passing on by parents to their children of what they know to be the case. We begin by trusting our parents and, by extension, our elders generally. Many of the things they tell us we can presume they know, but if we accept them our reason is that our parents said so. Eventually their hope would be that we will come to hold those things without the sanction of parental authority. Now it makes a great deal of difference what we are told at the outset, how we are brought up. Indeed, as Aristotle remarked, it makes all the difference.[4] If we have a well-ordered view of life, we want to pass that on to our children and we would bitterly resent it if someone else undertook to tell our children to act in a way contrary to that in which we are bringing them up. We could of course argue the point with a peer, but we don't argue with our children; we persuade and cajole, we tell them things for their own good, etc. Without a certain kind of disposition inculcated from an early age, it is unlikely that children would grow up to see certain truths about life. There are, in short, subjective dispositions necessary for seeing the way things are in the moral order.

Now something remotely similar to this is operative at the beginning of our formal study of philosophy. Dispositions are acquired, attitudes taken on, which have an influence that is or can be quite far-reaching. All this is on the periphery of philosophy itself, of course, but it is part and parcel of philosophizing. That is a point to which we shall return later, but perhaps enough has been said to indicate why one can be reasonably chary of the contention that it really doesn't matter where we begin the study of philosophy or how.

Philosophy and Philosophizing

I want now to make explicit a distinction that has been operative in the foregoing pages, a distinction of which we have particular need at this juncture. Our talk of learning and tradition and even of the trust which characterizes the beginning of our formal study of philosophy laid heavy stress on the objectivity of knowledge. What is known is not a personal possession of teacher or learner because it reflects the way things are. That objective reference of knowledge is what permits the learner to separate himself from the trust and faith without which he could hardly begin. This emphasis permits us to speak of philosophy as something autonomous and objective, almost as if it were out-there, independent of human minds. This suggestion could be exaggerated in a way that would make the matter utterly ridiculous, of course; without human minds there would simply be no philosophy. What we wanted to stress, and what must be stressed, is that the criterion of knowledge is the real, that human minds which do philosophy are measured by the way things are, rather than vice versa. The ancients, notably Aristotle, likened the human mind to a simple capacity or potentiality, but a potentiality for all things; in knowledge it is as if the whole of reality could become present to us, that we could, in some sense, become all things.[5] This is not to say that the mind does not contribute to the activity we call knowing. Categories, generalizations, all manners of relations are attributed to things which belong to them only insofar as they are known by us. Man does not exist, only individual men, and although there is a warrant in things for the universal nature the mind enunciates, nothing outside the mind answers *as such* to human nature conceived as some one thing relating to many individuals. One of Aristotle's complaints against Plato was that he failed to distinguish what belongs to things in themselves and what belongs to them as a consequence of our knowing them. The Platonic idea, Aristotle felt, is merely a projection outside the mind of the universals we form in knowing the individuals in the world. This is an extremely vexed topic, of course, and we mention it now because it provides a first reminder that, even when we stress the objectivity of knowledge, the fact that the real is the measure of true knowledge, we do so out of an awareness that there is a subjective side to knowledge.

The subjective side of knowledge to which we have just drawn attention, that which consists of the relations that attach to things as a result of our knowing them, is what Aristotle meant by logic.[6] It is perfectly possible to have objective knowledge of this subjective complement or component of knowledge, moreover, and while Aristotle would not have thought that the logician was studying things out-there, he would certainly have insisted that the logician is not concerned with the private or arbitrary, with what is subjective in various stronger senses, say mine as opposed to yours. But there is a far wider context to the knowledge that makes up philosophy, a context which calls our attention to the subject who is engaged in this study. To study philosophy is a human act and now, when we want to speak of this human activity, we will employ the term "philosophizing" to designate it.[7] While philosophizing is on the side of the subject and thus may be termed the subjective aspect of philosophy, it is nonetheless something which can be generalized and communicated. It is the objective or shareable aspects of this subjectivity we want to examine now.

Kierkegaard is often looked upon as the opponent of speculative or theoretical thought and consequently of much that has gone by the name philosophy.[8] Actually, this is not wholly true; indeed, when one reflects on Kierkegaard's criticisms of what he calls, variously, Pure Thought, Abstract Thought, and Speculative Thought, it becomes clear that what he is calling attention to is the rather obvious fact that thought involves a thinker. In short, he is inviting us to make just the shift we are trying to make with our distinction between philosophy and philosophizing. As a matter of fact, much of what I want now to propose has been heavily influenced by some fifteen years of study in Kierkegaard. Having said that, however, I want to begin by calling attention to a passage in Aristotle, the ultimate significance of which can easily be overlooked.

At the outset of his *Metaphysics*, Aristotle attempts to assign a meaning to the term "wisdom" which will enable him to convey what he means by "philosophy," the etymology of which is, of course, the love or pursuit of wisdom. Aristotle has something rather remote and sophisticated in mind when he uses the term "wisdom" to define philosophy, and it is for that very reason that he is intent on attaching his somewhat far-out use of the term to everyday experience and ordinary language. In doing this he gives a kind of panoramic sketch of the ground out of which metaphysics comes. (That is a deliberate invocation of Heidegger.) The much quoted opening sentence of the *Metaphysics* is, "All men by nature desire to see or know." That assertion is at once controversial and self-evident. Controversial, if by knowing we think of what goes on in Plato's academy or a modern university and so forth; rather difficult to quarrel with if by knowing we mean, first of all, something as basic as sense perception. Well, it is to sense perception that Aristotle first appeals, and the knowledge or awareness gained by the senses is quickly attached to its practical utility. The senses are instruments without which animals could not get along in this world and, insofar as the value of getting along in this world is an unquestioned assumption of animal life, we can emend Aristotle's opening to make it read, All animals desire to know. To be sure, even when speaking of the external senses, Aristotle introduces his major theme by observing that we take particular delight in seeing *even when it is not ordered to some practical end*, but apart from that his discussion proceeds with continuing reference to what he considers man shares with animals and, when he moves to peculiarly human activities, his emphasis is on the practical. Of course, in man, sensation has a two-fold function; it is necessary for survival and thus has a practical ordination and it is the root of experience out of which knowledge arises and thus has ultimately a theoretical ordination. But it is know-how that is first gained, cognitive attitudes which enable man to survive, which enable him to establish a society of his fellows and to gain some measure of surcease from the struggle to live. It is with the advent of leisure that theoretical knowledge of a more or less disinterested character becomes a possibility.

What has this to do with our present inquiry? This, I think, that we can consider each man as recapitulating what Aristotle there describes in terms of social history. Man is a being in the world, he is there among things, and this fact calls for any number of adjustments and attitudes before he undertakes the formal study of philosophy. One does not have to go the whole distance, with Marx, and say that philosophy is merely an ideology created by the practical and economic order, but surely it is true to say that we come to the formal study of philosophy against the background of a long, practical involvement in the world. I am not suggesting that this involvement is mindless; it is here that, by and large, I would

locate what we spoke of earlier as common sense; it is here
that we acquire both the irrefragable certitudes which no
later thought can undermine as well as the myths and emotive interpretations which seem to have as their major purpose to make us at home in the world.

We have already referred to discussions of the historical
origins of philosophy out of myth. It has been said that myth
is not something which is surpassed once for all, and I would
like to turn that suggestion into a reminder that philosophy
is but one way of comporting ourselves vis-à-vis reality. Some
contemporary thinkers, like Heidegger, have attempted to analyze what it means to be human in the broadest of senses
and, if that could be done, doing philosophy might be seen as
simply one way of being human, not the first way and, humanly speaking, not the most satisfactory way.[9]

But who in the world would have to be reminded of that?
Many philosophers, as it turns out, philosophers who apparently feel they are speaking of man's original and fundamental
involvement in the world when they discuss esoteric epistemological problems. Is the objective reality of physical objects the sort of question a man might first ask? By first here
we mean chronologically first, that is, as a child or, if you
prefer, as primitive man. To imagine this is absurd. We accept the world as where we are; we relate to objects as
things to be desired and avoided; we learn to walk and talk
and act in myriad ways. All this is simply given; it can neither
be questioned by doubt nor constituted by philosophical
thought. At the outset, our energies are devoted to keeping
a foothold in a world which is indisputably there. Survival
may, in certain cultures, be less of a problem than in others,
but it is always with some degree of effort that we do survive. Now what I get out of such reminders as these, reminders which come most often from those philosophers who

are called existentialists, is that man is basically an agent, an actor. Isn't that the import of the first chapter of Aristotle's *Metaphysics?* Kierkegaard expressed it by saying that man is not basically a knowing subject but an ethical subject, for him to exist is, first of all, basically, and this means from first to last, a matter of becoming what he ought to be.[10] That is the basic configuration of human life and it is into it that we have to place man as knower. A man knows in a context. The knower is an existing man.

The reminder of the human condition which we find in existentialism, particularly in Kierkegaard, has import for both philosophy and philosophizing. Although it is the latter which principally interests us now, a brief word may be said of the former. If man is first of all a doer, if knowledge as it first arises in him is ordered to goods that he more or less automatically seeks, this will have an impact on the more formal pursuit of knowledge which he may undertake with age and leisure. A man struggling to survive could hardly be expected to be assailed by epistemological problems concerning the reality of the external world. Such problems would seem unreal to him, phony, faintly decadent, and in large part he would be right. Right because he is involved in the world in the fundamental way that man is always involved in it, the way in which our first confused certitudes are gained, certitudes that no later experience, no matter how sophisticated, can gainsay, because however obliquely and surreptitiously, it is to this basic experience that all human activity refers. The solipsist voices his theory and writes it down and if hypocrisy is the compliment vice pays to virtue, communication is the fatal concession skepticism pays to realism. In short, our philosophical theories, as we earlier urged, have to be in contact with the ineradicable element of common sense; philosophy must begin with those confused certitudes and in large part what it is after is clarification as to what those certitudes bear on. The plain man is certain he is alive and that a live man differs from a dead one; he is right even though he would be unable to state what precisely the difference consists of. After centuries of study, perhaps no one can yet state that difference in a wholly satisfactory way. But the living are no less different from the dead; that certitude does not waver in the real world, whatever its fate in some classrooms.[11]

To turn now to philosophizing, we want to examine the implications of the fact that the pursuit of knowledge is a moral act. This seems an odd statement, of course, because we normally want to distinguish between becoming knowledgeable and becoming good. One can be quite expert at geometry and be for all that a deficient human person. Moreover, we don't have to contrast moral action and such abstract knowledge as geometry to see the difference. It is one of the more poignant facts of life that one can know what he ought to do and yet not do it; moral knowledge, knowledge of moral values and rules, must be distinguished from moral action. This is not to say that action is blind and unthinking, but that the knowledge operative in our deeds is different from the reflective knowledge of human action which makes up moral philosophy or ethics. So let us put our opening point this way: the study of ethics is a moral act.

Where does this lead us? If we are seeking knowledge we are seeking something that is a good where by good we mean something perfective of us. Knowledge perfects our mind; knowledge is a good. The point of our distinction between philosophy and philosophizing is that it enables us to see that the activity in which we seek the good of knowledge is but one human activity, that there are goods other than the good of knowledge, that criteria for the pursuit of goods can be recognized and that thereby the pursuit of knowledge is brought within a very broad category of human activity in general. What we should expect, and what it has been argued does emerge, is a hierarchy of values or goods. How then does the good of knowledge compare with the other goods of man? If we revert to Aristotle, we must come up with a double answer here. Let us give the usual answer first. It is characteristic of man that he seeks knowledge for its own sake; thanks to his reason, man's cognitive involvement is qualitatively different from that of other cosmic things. Man, the old definition runs, is a rational animal. Well, then, if reason is man's defining characteristic, the good of reason must be the most appropriate good for man to seek. Now it is interesting that when Aristotle arrives at this point he dwells on the ambiguity of "good of reason."[12] Can't man's rational activity be various things, he asks, can't it mean the perfection of reasoning just as such, on the one hand, and, on the other, the perfection of other activities insofar as they come under the sway of reason? Both the geometer and the carpenter are engaged in rational activity when they perform their proper tasks, but "rational activity" means different things in the two cases. The carpenter is reasoning about activities other than reasoning, he is putting his mind to the driving of nails, the planing of boards, the erection of walls, etc. The geometer accomplishes his task if the reasoning process itself is performed well. Now I want to take the geometer as a symbol of disinterested knowledge, not that the geometer is without interest in knowledge, but that geo-metrical knowledge is not as such a measure of an activity other than thinking. That is all that is meant by saying that geometrical knowledge is theoretical or disinterested. The rational activity of the carpenter involves a knowledge directive of activities other than thinking, the goal of which activities is, say, sheltering man from the elements. The rational activity of artisans and practical men can be thought of as directed to the most basic goods: survival, food, shelter, etc. These are goods with which man is first of all concerned, with which he must always be concerned. Not only must he seek them, he must seek them in a proper way; not only must he act, he must act well. As a social being he must perform his activities in the light of his relations with others, his family, his neighbors, his city, his country, etc.

It would be best, of course, if we prolonged this discussion to develop the criteria for doing such deeds well. That is not our precise task now, but we rely on the reader's ability to recognize that even when the carpenter is performing his task as carpenter well we can still say that he shouldn't be doing what he is doing. If he is building barracks at Dachau, for example, few of us would want to marvel at the finesse with which he planes and hammers and saws; we would want to say he shouldn't be doing that. I think we could develop reasons to underpin those judgments. We shall attempt to do this, not in the case of carpentry, but in the case of doing philosophy.

Is it possible to ask how one should go about the study of philosophy where the criteria appealed to when we say the student is performing his task well are not just as such the criteria of the knowledge he is trying to acquire? That is, what would it mean to say that one who is learning geometry and well is not acting as he should? We are thinking of learning here on an analogy with the case of the man who performs well as a carpenter but badly as a man where the different judgments bear on the same act. One can fiddle well while Rome burns. What we have been getting at in this circuitous way is this question: what if any is the relation between moral virtue and the intellectual life, appetitive dispositions and the perfection of the mind?

The Ethics of Philosophizing

Our problem could be approached in terms of an issue of current importance, namely, the moral responsibilities of the scientist. Think of the chemist who with great finesse perfects a gas the sole function of which is to destroy life. What is the relation of knowledge to other values, moral values? In working toward a position with regard to such a problem, we must implicitly at least make a judgment on the way in which values other than purely cognitive ones can or cannot take precedence over them. What we were trying to suggest earlier is that such a problem seemingly ought not arise if by definition man is the animal who seeks knowledge and if, accordingly, moral appraisals are to be made with reference to the cognitive good. That is, if the good of knowledge is the overriding good for man, how could any other good take precedence over it and lead to the conclusion that, in given circumstances, the good of knowledge ought not be sought? Let us rediscover the problem in less exalted circumstances. Consider a man who pursues knowledge to the detriment of his health. One who holds that physical well-being is a lesser good than the good of cognitive truth could nevertheless chide another who endangers his health by his pell-mell pursuit of knowledge and, if asked to give the grounds for his reprimand, he would not of course say that health is a greater good than knowledge, but rather something like, without physical well-being you will not long be able to pursue the good of knowledge. In short, health is a condition for the acquisition of the greater good and one might even say that, in certain circumstances, the lesser good would take precedence over the greater good because of one's long-term interest in the greater good. Perhaps this enables us to see how things other than knowledge, goods less than the good of knowledge which is truth, can condition our appraisals of modes of pursuing the greater good. Once more, there is no need to question the absolute hierarchy of values, no need to say that something other than the perfection of man's defining capacity is really man's greater good. Rather, by taking into account the conditions and context of the pursuit of the good, one may, in a foreshortened perspective, seem to rule against the greater good, whereas, in the long haul, it is precisely one's concern for the greater good that explains the appraisal.

Now something like these considerations underlies the old adage *primum vivere, deinde philosophare*: live first, thence philosophize. This adage, like most adages, is susceptible of any number of interpretations. It could be taken to recommend experience prior to reflection on experience. It could be understood, as it was understood by Unamuno, as a reversal of the Greek hierarchy of values, so that the measure of the worth of knowledge is its import and value for the supreme value, life.[18] But of course if it is a question of human life, as it is for Unamuno, we must ask what the defining characteristics of human life are and we may come up with the Greek answer. To return for a moment to Aristotle at the beginning of his *Metaphysics*, we might want to say that nothing is more desirable than wisdom, since nothing else is more perfective of man, and yet nothing is less necessary than wisdom.[14] What Aristotle seems to be getting at is the priority of the conditions of philosophy. Until life is secure, at least to some degree, the pursuit of theoretical knowledge will simply not be a live issue. That is why the practical activities with reference to which Aristotle begins his discussion of man's natural desire for knowledge take chronological precedence over the theoretical; the necessities of life are not merely necessary conditions for any less interested human activity, as for example the fine arts and theoretical knowledge, they are necessities as well in the sense that here man is not free, is bound. This seems to underlie the designation of some of these activities as servile arts and the servility in question is not unrelated to the needs and demands of the body. Once these necessities were secured, man was free for other pursuits, for pursuits which came to be called liberal: the liberal arts, the *artes humaniores* or humanities, were more typically human not because they were more basic but because they were more proportionate to man's defining spiritual element.

The chronological priority of goods less than man's chief good is the basis for appraisals which favor these goods over the purely cognitive good although, as we have suggested, the ultimate ground of such appraisals may very well be the cognitive good which is temporarily and teleologically overridden. Later we will want to indicate other corollaries of this chronological priority of goods man shares with lesser creatures, corollaries more intrinsically relevant to philosophy since they have to do with theory of knowledge and philosophical terminology. For the moment, the point we have been trying to make can be summarized in the following way. In discussing philosophizing, the process whereby we pursue knowledge and truth, reference is made to goods extrinsic to philosophy, to goods other than the perfection of the mind, and appraisals made. The pursuit of knowledge as a human activity must be undertaken with regard to goods and values other than the good of knowledge itself. This does not entail that these other goods thereby become intrinsic to philosophy, but respect for them, taking them into account, is essential to philosophizing. This is what we meant by saying that philosophizing is a human act and that it involves judgments which are essentially moral.

Since it is a topic which is seldom discussed nowadays,[15] although this was not always the case, we wish to devote a few lines to the relationship between moral goodness and the intellectual life. The strongest way to raise the question is to ask whether a bad man could be a good moral philosopher, but rather than treat the subject abstractly, we shall do so by reference to Plato's *Phaedo*.

The setting of this dialogue of Plato is the death cell of Socrates and the question of the dialogue centers on the immortality of the soul. In a discussion which attaches to attempts to prove the soul's immortality, Socrates and his friends discuss the philosopher and philosophy. We are there given a description of philosophy which seldom fails to surprise the reader. Philosophy, we are told, is the study of death, a preparation for death, a kind of mimicking of the condition of the dead. In order to grasp the meaning of this seemingly bizarre description, we must recall the main lines of Plato's thoughts on knowledge. Plato held that truly to know is to know what cannot be otherwise; that is, the object of knowledge must be unchanging and necessary. If this were not so, we could claim to know something which by the morrow would be otherwise than we thought it to be. One has only to consider mathematics to gather Plato's point. If one has achieved a geometrical demonstration he can express a statement and the reasons for it and what he says is considered not simply to have been that way, it is not merely thought that it will be that way; rather, one judges that it *is* that way, timelessly, unchangeably, and so forth. Since Plato had no doubt that knowledge in this strict sense is possible, he had only to isolate its objects. Two possible candidates are rejected. First of all, Plato takes it to be quite obvious that the sensible things of this world cannot be objects of knowledge in the full sense. Sensible, physical things are by definition changeable things—Plato goes so far as to say, in the *Theaetetus*, that they are in a constant state of flux, even that they are flux. Second, it might occur to us that our concepts are what we know and that these have sufficient fixity and freedom from change to be deemed necessary. Plato gives this suggestion no serious attention at all and when it is put forward in the *Parmenides* he simply rejects it. Perhaps it was because our concepts are formed, come to be, and can subsequently be lost or forgotten that Plato dismissed them as grounds of knowledge in the strict sense. At any rate, dismiss them he did and if he were going to retain his belief that we can have knowledge in the strict sense, he had to seek its objects elsewhere than in physical things or in mental concepts. In some such way we can imagine the Platonic doctrine of forms or ideas emerging. When in learning geometry we come to know truths about the triangle, the object of this knowledge is neither the figure drawn in the sand nor our mental image. It is triangle, of course, even *the* triangle or triangularity that we know and that is something immaterial, changeless, necessary. Plato knows where it is not and what it is not and that is sufficient: he can say of it that it is separate, that is, elsewhere. The very heart of Plato's philosophy is here; he has no doubt that there are objects of knowledge, the forms or ideas. He is aware of the difficulties of the doctrine; he says in the Seventh Letter that nowhere has he written down a proof of their existence. More often than not, what he will say is that, unless there are ideas, knowledge and philosophy would be impossible—which he takes to be a *reductio ad absurdum*.

What has this to do with the description of philosophy as the study of death or with our larger question of the relation between morality and knowledge? Sensible things are not objects of knowledge for Plato; they may be occasions of knowledge, reminding us of the idea or form they faintly imitate. Sensible things are objects of perception or sensation and Plato sets up a proportionality, Sensation : Sensible things :: Knowledge : Ideas. This has as a result the linking of sensible things and body, on the one hand, and ideas with mind or soul. Furthermore, in the *Phaedo*, Plato may be seen to use sensation in an ambiguous way; it is not only perception of physical things, it is also sensuality, the desire for, the tendency toward physical things. But the appetitive move toward the things of this world binds us to them, makes us like them, clouds the eye of the soul so that it becomes blind to true reality, the realm of the ideas. Well, we can see the consequence. In order to achieve true knowledge, we must turn away from sensation, both in its cognitive aspect as perception and in its emotive or passional aspect as sensuality. The seeker of knowledge must conquer the body; therefore, he must acquire moral virtue which seems to be for Plato a kind of suppression of the corporeal. Thus, the philosopher in whom the soul has achieved independence of and separation from the body is like the dead, that is, like the released soul, freed from its incarceration in the body. Of course, this can be achieved only imperfectly in this life, so the soul of the philosopher longs for the full freedom of death.

All of this is well known to readers of Plato, of course, but what do we make of it? There are a number of clichés often invoked to defuse Plato's message: For the Greeks, philosophy was a way of life; the *Phaedo* exhibits in a striking way the Pythagorean influence on Plato; we are faced here with the religious as opposed to the scientific strand in Greek thought. And so forth. All too often these clichés are taken to explain something, even to explain it away. The final remark, for instance, suggests that poor Plato had not yet traveled an adequate distance from the myth and theology out of which philosophy arose. The first two remarks can have a double import. First, they can be used to stress the fact that for Christians *the* way of life could no longer be what philosophy meant for the Greeks. Second, and this is never really developed, so far as I know, the suggestion seems to be that we in our wisdom have succeeded in isolating philosophy from a moral context, that for us philosophy is an expertise which can be gained regardless of one's moral condition and carried on perfectly well in utter independence of one's moral character. We will be returning in a moment to the problem of Christianity and philosophy, but now we want to examine the view that philosophy is a morally neutral expertise.

Let us begin by stressing the plausibility of the position. Isn't it the case that one can be a perfectly good mathematician and a reprehensible man? There has been much discussion of the artist in this regard. To be a good artist and to be a good man are clearly not one and the same thing. Well, isn't the same true of the mathematician, the physicist, the biologist, etc.? An affirmative answer seems demanded and, with few qualifications, we give an affirmative answer to the question. The qualifications are nonetheless important. Whether or not the scientist is morally good, in order for him to be a scientist, to learn science, to carry on as a scientist, he must continually make moral judgments that are relevant to his pursuit of scientific knowledge. In short, our concession is simply that the scientist may be morally bad, not that to be a scientist is utterly independent, for this man, from a whole host of moral judgments. In the case of the artist, for example, we often speak of great sacrifices made for art and surely part of what we are saying is that he makes judgments, arranges his life practically with reference to his art, and that these judgments are not of the same sort as those he makes when he is making an artifact. To spell this out: to decide to live in a garret, to decide against marriage and family life, for the sake of one's art, is not the same kind of judgment the painter makes when he is composing a picture and chooses this color, this arrangement, and so forth. It is not the canons of art which are appealed to in the choice of a garret (one could get the north light on the first floor), in eschewing marriage, and the like. It is not the principles of physics which govern the choice of DuPont over MIT, Notre Dame over Cape Kennedy, etc. These practical decisions are made with reference to moral principles and they may be good or bad, more or less good and more or less bad; moreover, at least within a given range, they need not affect the knowing and judgments which do make reference to the principles of the science.

As a first step, then, we can say that the perfection of knowledge can be achieved without dependence on moral goodness. This does not mean, however, that the attainment of knowledge, the pursuit of knowledge, is an activity that can be detached from a whole host of practical judgments, many of them moral, all of them susceptible of extra-scientific appraisal. As a second step in this inquiry, let us consider whether or not moral turpitude, which is extrinsic to knowledge in the sense of science, can be inimical to the achievement or practice of science. This is to come at the problem by the back door, but negatives often have a way of illumining the positive. Surely, as soon as we ask the question, the answer comes crowding in. A thoroughly intemperate man, a drunk, could be because of his vice incapable of carrying on in the laboratory. An artist who becomes culpably addicted to drugs might find the practice of his art difficult; he might become so indifferent to it that he forgets all about it. Less dramatic vices can have their influence on the intellectual life; vices such as vanity blind us to flaws in our own views, make us impervious to pertinent criticism and determined to defend our own views at all costs, whatever the evidence and arguments. There is no need to labor the point. It is quite evident that moral vice, which is not just as such an intellectual fault, in the sense that it is quite different from falsehood, can have a deleterious effect on the intellectual life, can impede our achievement of the perfection of knowledge.

With this as background, we can perhaps regain the Platonic or, more generally, the Greek vantage point. If moral vice can have the effect of impeding our quest for knowledge, can moral virtue facilitate this quest? Plato's position can perhaps best be arrived at in this fashion. Granted that to be a good mathematician is not just as such to be a good man and granted, too, that to be a good man is not tantamount to being a good mathematician, is it not the case nevertheless that the ideal combination would be that of the good man and the good mathematician? It seems that Plato, and Aristotle, too, found it difficult to grasp the idea that a man might seriously seek the perfection of knowledge without at the same time concerning himself with the perfection of his choices and practical decisions. An historical basis for their tendency to wed the two concerns can be found in their attitude toward the Sophist; both men saw in sophistry the perversion of the intellectual by bad desire, the desire for fame, the desire to win the argument, the desire for money. This would suggest that one must desire the truth well, desire knowledge well, since to desire it badly, immoderately, unvirtuously led to the defeat of the desire. Notice that this means that not only should desires for goods other than knowledge be moderated, that is, become subject to virtue, but that even our desire for and pursuit of knowledge should become subject of virtue. This is not simply a plea for intellectual virtue, that is, the determination of thinking toward its proper object, truth, but a plea for moral virtues which have a special relevance for the intellectual life.

The Virtues of the Intellectual

Once one thinks about it, there is surely nothing surprising in the suggestion that one's moral attitudes are influential in the pursuit of knowledge. When we exhort students to read carefully, to avoid precipitous judgments or to concentrate their efforts rather than disperse them, we are commending attitudes which can safely be called moral. Young people are urged to acquire good study habits, to discipline themselves and dispose their time prudently. As it happens, scattered through Aquinas' *Summa theologiae* are a number of discussions having to do with moral attitudes important for the acquisition of intellectual perfection. For example, when Aquinas is talking about prudence or practical wisdom (Aristotle's *phronesis*), he introduces the notion of docility. His interest in it is chiefly with respect to its necessity for moral virtue and he emphasizes the benefit to be gained from listening to and learning from our elders in making practical decisions. Nevertheless, he alludes to its importance for the acquisition of intellectual virtue.[16] His discussion of precipitousness also has rather obvious application to their intellectual order.[17] But without a doubt the most interesting and important discussions for our purposes are those concerned with studiousness and curiosity. The first of these is an instance of temperance which is generically a moderation of appetite or desire. This moderation is necessary, Aquinas suggests, lest we desire to excess what we naturally desire; he gives as examples our natural desire for food and drink. Then, citing the opening sentence of the *Metaphysics*, that all men by nature desire to know, Aquinas says that studiousness is precisely the moderation of this natural desire.[18] The immoderate desire for knowledge is what Aquinas means by curiosity and his discussion of this vice, opposed to the virtue of studiousness, is of particular interest to us at this juncture.[19]

Reminding us that studiousness is not directly related to knowledge itself, but rather to the pursuit of and desire for knowledge, since judgments about knowledge are one thing and judgments about its pursuit another, St. Thomas points out that knowledge of the truth is just as such a good for man. The reasoning behind this is the teleology of man's defining capacity which is reason; its actualization, its perfection or good, is precisely knowledge of the truth. But, while of itself good, knowledge of the truth can be accidentally bad by reason of its consequences—if it is the occasion for pride and vanity, for example. Aquinas cites the *Epistle to the Corinthians* (VIII.1), *scientia inflat:* knowledge puffs up. Furthermore, if one uses knowledge for a bad purpose, the knowledge could be judged accidentally bad. Now Aquinas is not concerned with knowledge so regarded in his discussion of curiosity; it is not knowledge but the desire and pursuit of knowledge which is the locus for studiousness and curiosity.

The basic assumption here is that the desire or pursuit of

truth can be well ordered or perverse. In connection with the foregoing, St. Thomas observes that one might pursue knowledge because of some consequence of its possession, which consequence is evil. Thus, I might seek knowledge in order to lord it over my fellows, in order to take pride in it and to consider myself not like the rest of men. Furthermore, I might seek to acquire some knowledge or expertise in order to achieve monetary success and, with it, a pagan mode of existence. At the outset, then, Aquinas speaks of a vicious desire for knowledge which is such, not because knowledge is evil, but because what one is really seeking is a reprehensible concomitant of knowledge.

Having made this point, Aquinas goes on to discuss four ways in which a moral fault arises from an inordinate desire for learning truth. The *first* may be described as a violation of the principle, first things first. Aquinas quotes St. Jerome lamenting priests whose principal interest is secular drama and amorous and bucolic songs to the detriment of their knowledge of Scripture. Because of their office, priests take on obligations with respect to possible objects of knowledge, some knowledge being more incumbent upon them than other, and a violation of this order is blameworthy. Imagine a priest who need cede to no one in knowledge of the James Bond novels but who referred you to a Scripture scholar when you asked him about the Gospel. Imagine a man who had contracted to teach physics and who devotes the bulk of his time to a translation of Catullus begun in prep school to the detriment of the field in which he has engaged himself to excel.

A *second* example of inordinate desire for knowledge is the pursuit of illicit knowledge, e.g., astrology. The appraisal of knowledge as illicit is made here by appeal to faith, and Aquinas quotes Augustine as wondering whether some philosophers are not impeded from believing because of their interest in demons and spirits. Knowledge of the occult, whether judged to be nonsense from a religious or from another point of view, is sought after culpably. I suppose we would say, in a secular vein, that one is wasting his time, perverting the proper use of his mind, if he spends his days trying to predict the future or to make contact with spirits or to devise a foolproof gambling system. Aquinas' *third* example of curiosity—and we are here faced with an assessment which may seem to be properly religious although it is in keeping with the Greek conception of philosophy—is one who seeks knowledge of creatures without referring that knowledge to their creator. We might say that a deliberate and a priori restriction of intellectual interest to the finite, to the neutral, existentially speaking, is regarded as a vice by Aquinas. Such a judgment involves an attitude toward the whole context of man's pursuit of knowledge. Why is man a knower? Why has he been given this capacity? What is the ultimate import of his natural desire to know? If that desire cannot be pursued pell-mell, as it cannot, to what do we appeal in directing it? In doing so, we are making normative judgments whose function is to guide a reflective quest of knowledge, and here attitudes toward the hierarchy of objects of knowledge are inevitable. We may seem to be confining ourselves to proximate and pragmatic criteria when we give advice to others as to the order they should follow in study. The objective that may guide our advice could be academic (you need three more credits to graduate) or the broader and more remote target of career and income (philosophy majors usually end up on the dole), but Aquinas invites our attention to more encompassing criteria. It is as if there is involved in the immediate rules and guidelines we may suggest at least an implicit attitude toward what man is, what life is all about. In its original scope philosophy had as a task to explore just such questions and the answers to them control advice one would give a beginner concerning the motivation for philosophizing. We may be made uneasy by the suggestion that our advice to the young presupposes that we have made such inquiries, but if we have not, how do we justify our justifications for this line of study or that? In all kinds of ways, certainly, which in a foreshortened perspective function adequately enough. But the question, "Why should I seek knowledge at all?" is a good one and we must think of it as raised by one actually pursuing knowledge, one who has felt the attraction of truth, if we are to appreciate how interesting the question is. We will be returning to this third instance of curiosity mentioned by Aquinas when we raise explicitly the question of what relation should obtain between divine faith and the pursuit of knowledge.

A *fourth* and final instance of the inordinate pursuit of knowledge is one who seeks knowledge beyond his proper capacities. One of the tasks of graduate faculties is to warn ill-equipped aspirants away from an area of scholarship. A student may have the will, the desire, but when his professors become rather sure that he has not the talent to justify pursuing the desire, they will tell him to turn his efforts in another direction. If such a student should ignore qualified advice and the significance of experienced failure, we would rightly feel his continued quest has the makings of a moral fault.

I suspect that the preceding will strike as strange what we vaguely call the modern mind. It is relatively easy, as I have tried to do, to turn the types of curiosity Aquinas mentions into descriptions of rather readily recognizable phenomena. The man who ignores his contractual obligations and devotes his energies and time as an amateur to a field other than his professional one; the man who wastes his time seeking a kind of knowledge which, by one criterion or another, we judge to be illicit or non-existent; the man who persists in the study of a subject he has not the wit to master—we have all, alas, encountered such men. *We* might write them off as neurotic and they may be neurotic; Aquinas tends to regard such mistakes first of all as instances of morally culpable desire. The latter may lead to the former; we may be faced with a subtle mixture of the two. But surely it should not strain our imagination to see that there may be reasons short of mental illness to explain why a person acts in violation of what is for us common sense. He just may be morally culpable and deserving of blame. He may, of course, be me and, while I am reluctant to impute blame to others, I would prefer to regard myself as morally at fault rather than the victim of putative forces over which I have no control. Think of this discussion as a self-examination and we break down the resistance we may have to seeing that in our pursuit of knowledge things may not be as they ought to be.

Interim Summary

Before turning to the problem toward which this whole chapter has been tending, the problem which is summarized in the phrase Christian Philosophy, let us recapitulate briefly what has gone before. I wanted to say that, in order to begin the study of philosophy, at least when the beginning is not a matter of mere chance, we tend to take the advice of others as to the best way to begin, or at least a good and possible way of beginning. This does not mean, of course, that we are terribly conscious of what we are doing; it does not mean that we reflect on the fact that we are trusting others and assess the reasonableness of doing so. But we can look back on the fact and see that that is indeed what we were doing and can then judge that it was reasonable to do so. Part of the reasonableness of trust resides in its inevitability, of course, but then we didn't follow just any advice. We didn't stop strangers on the street and ask them where we should go to school or what courses we should enroll in. More likely, we trusted people whose recognized function it is to give such advice. We may seek advice about advisers, and it would be the rare student who doesn't, but this is to enlarge the circle of advisers rather than to break out of it. If it is reasonable to trust others as to how we should begin the study of philosophy, the reasons which constitute this reasonableness are not just as such philosophical reasons. What we are taking advice on is where we might go to get philosophical reasons. In short, I wanted to argue that, when we think of philosophizing, the study of philosophy, rather than of philosophy just as such, we are inevitably in an area where pre-philosophical or extra-philosophical reasons are essentially involved and that these reasons govern decisions we make concerning the deployment of time and effort. Should we confine ourselves to the condition of those who seek to learn in academe, we are confronted with a pretty universal and common and unavoidable situation where trust is the mark of the tyro. It is with reference to this common situation that we will want to discuss the specific situation of the student in a Catholic college.

Having opened the way to a distinction between philosophy and philosophizing, where the latter term covered a host of human acts which are the concrete context of philosophy, the decisions whereby we pursue the knowledge which constitutes philosophy, we wanted to go the whole distance and consider the moral overtones of philosophizing. This we regarded as a discussion which is nowadays unusual although in ancient and medieval times it was introduced without fanfare and apology as an obvious object of interest. The older and more commodious attitude involved talking of the relationship between moral virtue and vice and the acquisition or attainment of the object of study. We tried to remove some of the strangeness of such considerations by suggesting continuing concerns which answer to the older talk of the virtues and vices of the intellectual. In the course of transposing such matters into less alarming terminology, into everyday academic occurrences, we hoped to show that it is still a widespread practice to commend appropriate moral virtues (e.g., good study habits) and warn against certain vices (e.g., don't try to learn everything at once).

If there is an upshot to the foregoing, it is this. It is not peculiar to Catholics to recognize the importance of extra-philosophical criteria in talking about the learning of philosophy since some kind of trust or acceptance on the part of the student, based on principles other than those controlling a given subject matter, is a basic assumption of the organization of institutions of learning. Furthermore, though the roots of such advice may go unexamined, we do quite generally give advice to students that can only be called moral and which is given because of its peculiar relevance to the pursuit of knowledge.

Since what we are engaged on in this essay is, in great part, the setting down of truisms too easily forgotten, we are not in the least embarrassed by the recognition that what we have been describing is neither news nor surprising. The reader will of course appreciate that, insofar as the intellectual life is discussed as if it were the activity of a disembodied mind, an activity which somehow simply starts, perhaps from a presuppositionless beginning, we are confronted with something worse than fantasy. Worse, because, unlike fantasy, such talk is invariably dangerous, humanly dangerous. The pursuit of knowledge is a human activity and it must be discussed as a human activity; it takes place in a context where desires other than that for knowledge are operative and must be taken into account; it takes place against a background of a practical involvement in the world and that involvement has importance both for the initial questions of philosophy and for its terminology. A philosophical argument is valid, its conclusion true or false, independently of the vice or virtue of the knower, but the route to the argument involves any number of judgments and decisions which are essentially moral. We may not be sufficiently dismayed by the possibility that we may praise an argument and abhor the arguer; Plato and Aristotle seem disinclined to believe the possibility would often be realized. Certainly it would be an infrequent occurrence if we, like they, described philosophy in terms of man's quest for perfection and came to see how odious it is for a man to fail to be a good man and achieve, partially, his perfection as a knower.

Christian Philosophy

Extra-philosophical attitudes are constitutive of philosophizing if not of philosophy; one who sees the distinction between philosophy and philosophizing, and the inevitable influence of the latter on the former, is not going to be struck dumb by our asking what influence religious faith has on philosophy. If practical and moral attitudes have a generally recognized influence on our pursuit of knowledge, it is only to be expected that a commitment as total and all-embracing as religious belief will also have an influence. The impingement of faith on reason and vice versa has been one of the most discussed questions since the beginning of the Christian era, certainly, and while it may seem to have been resolved more or less satisfactorily in the so-called ages of faith, perhaps most articulately in the medieval period, the modern age of philosophy begins with explicit efforts to dissociate reason from faith and faith from reason with consequences for theology which are not difficult to descry and decry; that this may have had a deleterious effect on philosophy itself is the surprising suggestion of many who have argued, in recent years, for what they call Christian philosophy. As with the matter of perennial philosophy, which came up in the preceding chapter, we shall not attempt to confront the many positions on the nature of Christian philosophy one by one. Rather, having provided a sketch of the context of the discussion, we shall make soundings in the literature, and make suggestions of our own with respect to the possibility and even desirability of Christian philosophy.

At the outset of this chapter we spoke of faith in the broad sense of one man's trust in another. To believe, we pointed out, is both to believe someone and something. In this sense of believe, one can see that it would be odd to believe what one knows, since reliance on another's word for what one knows is superfluous or absurd. So, if to believe is to take someone's word as the warrant for holding something, we could, for purposes of illustration, say that the nexus between the predicate and subject of the statement expressing which is believed is not evidence, not the nature of the objects spoken about, but precisely another's assurance that a connection between the objects exists. If a chemist tells me a substance is composed of such-and-such elements, I, who have never made the analysis in question, can accept the statement as true. That is, believe it to be true. Let us pretend that I am capable of making the analysis involved and could, on demand, pass from belief to knowledge with respect to the statement in question. For one reason or another, we do not always make that transition; we are content to believe all kinds of things we could know. Life would be impossible without such beliefs; without the majority of them remaining terminal. Few of us will ever verify the map of our city let alone that of our state or country, but we are not visited by a sense of the riskiness of life when we give directions to travelers, including ourselves, on the basis of such maps. Many things we believe in this way are not verified by us due to physical difficulties, due to restricted travel or laboratory time. We may simply lack the talent or training to pass from belief to knowledge. Nevertheless, in principle at least, all such beliefs bear on truths knowable and not merely believable by men.

The Christian faith differs from faith or belief in the common meaning of the terms in several ways.[20] First of all, the one whom we believe is no mere man, but God revealing. Second, what we believe, in the strong sense here, is something we are incapable of knowing or understanding in this life. The Christian can be quite clear as to what he believes and equally clear that he does not understand it. For example, Jesus Christ is truly God and truly man. He died the death of a man and we can say, on that basis, that God died. But no orthodox Christian ever maintained that he understood the union in Christ of the divine and human natures. If he understood it, he would not have to believe it, but in this life the only basis for maintaining that Christ is both God and man is to believe, to take His word for it. So too to accept as true that there are three Persons in the Divine Nature can only be done on the basis of belief. No living man has ever understood the Trinity and no living man ever will. So the Christian believes God, believes Christ and the Church Christ founded, and what he believes is enunciated in creeds, discussed by theologians, and defined by the Church. If we consider the truths the Christian believes in believing God we are struck by the fact that they impinge upon and overlap and sometimes seem to come in conflict with what men know or claim to know apart from God's revelation. The purpose of human life, sanctions for human behavior, recommended modes of action, the import of the cosmos in its origin and destiny are merely some of the things about which the Christian has rather decided views on the basis of his faith. Obviously it is possible to have views on the same matters independently of faith, a kind of test of which is had by appeal to the philosophy of pagans, developed in ignorance of the Jewish religion and prior to the coming of Christ.

Out of the myriad consequences of these hints at difficulties, let us select several. What if we should say that, thanks to our Christian faith, we have a world view, theories of man and cosmos and the destiny of each, rules for behavior, a vast pattern of interpretation of reality. Like some of the early Fathers, we might then say that we possess, thanks to revelation, thanks to Christ, what the pagans sought and only imperfectly found, namely, a complete philosophy. On this view, Christian belief replaces philosophy so far as believers are concerned and any impulse to do what philosophers did, perhaps even to read their writings, must be regarded as a temptation. In Christ the believer has the Way, the Truth, and the Life. What possible need could he have for anything else?

On the other hand, one might regard Christianity as consisting of rituals and moral attitudes and a nest of odd propositions which are said to be true in some Pickwickian sense: they are true if you accept them but there is no evidence that really supports them, the believer insists, which can function apart from accepting the evidence as supporting the truths. The "truths" of faith thus seem a queer sort of unverifiable truth and, as such, one may either choose not to suppress his laughter and disdain or, in a mood of pluralistic liberalism, honor the right of others to believe in any nonsense they like so long as they recognize that beliefs have nothing to do with knowledge. Believers have been attracted by this possibility of a *modus vivendi* between faith and knowledge. Why not consider the two utterly heterogeneous and say that knowledge can neither support faith nor refute it? Faith is simply a quite different use of the mind, for the believer a higher use, for the critical non-believer a depraved or primitive one. But in any case the twain will never meet.

Where would this second possibility lead us? Well, we might say that we know and can prove that, for man, death is not the end, and that this is a statement which is utterly without connection with the Christian's belief that death will bring with it a judgment at which he will be held accountable for his deeds in life and which will decide his eternal happiness or unhappiness. But what if a philosopher claims to know and to be able to prove that death is the end, that he cannot recognize as even remotely meaningful contrary claims. Wouldn't the Christian who conceded the cogency of such discourse and nonetheless blissfully continued to believe that death is not the end seem odd? And I mean odd to other believers as well as to non-believers?

If among the things the Christian believes objects are mentioned which also come up in the discourse of non-believers, it seems fair to ask that the believer consider it something of a duty on his part to compare belief statements about a given object and knowledge statements about the same object, particularly when the statements seem at variance with one another. This is surely not a task that can be laid at the doorstep of the non-believer nor does it seem to be a task that can simply be shrugged off as a temptation or distraction. If only because it could distract someone else right out of his faith, the competent believer will see an obligation to discuss the matter. And, it is to be hoped, his discussion of the matter will make sense to the non-believer as well as to his fellow believers. Speaking as generically as we are, we may seem to be suggesting that all such inquiries could come out the same way. That is, one might expect that a believer who occupies himself with knowledge claims about objects concerning which he believes certain truths will inevitably say that nothing on the level of knowledge can really have the slightest influence on faith regardless of how the matter originally appeared. Now it is possible that this would often be the result of such an investigation, but I think there is something fishy about the claim that things will always turn out this way. I think we are right in thinking that some things we know or claim to know are related to what we believe, even though we would not want to say that what we know entails faith. The reason we would not want to say that knowledge entails faith is that then Christianity would seem to be parading itself as a body of knowledge acquired through their own efforts by a group of highly talented thinkers. All we have to do is remind ourselves of the group Christ surrounded himself with—and surrounds himself with today?—to see how preposterous that claim is. Faith is not an intellectual accomplishment that discriminates between men on the basis of natural talent. Men of great natural talent and men of little or no natural talent are at bottom equal with respect to the faith—unless we want to say, with

Kierkegaard, that it is more difficult for the talented rather
than less difficult.[21] Christ rose from the dead. Why not? He
is God and God made the world and surely rising from
the dead is less difficult than making the living and non-living
from nothing. But this invocation of God's act as artificer
of the universe is an appeal to an immensely difficult matter,
perhaps as dark from the point of view of accessibility to
our minds as the Resurrection. In either case, creation in time
or the resurrection of the dead, we are presented with claims
which boggle the mind. The believer who has the time and
the talent will, in meditating on what he believes, inevitably
try to put it into relation with what he knows. He believes
without question that the world is totally dependent on the
creative act of God. But what precisely does that mean?
And, if the world is God's artifact, will not he as believer feel
a special impulse to want to know as much about it as he can?
It would be hard to document the reality of that impulse historically, of course, but what about now? Is science saying
things about the same world the believer holds is the effect
of God? Well, what does "same" mean here, and, if there
are different "worlds," what do we mean by "different" and
how do they compare?

If philosophy is defined in terms of knowledge gained with
reference only to principles available to the human mind
without special divine aid and if, on the other hand, the
knowledge of faith is precisely dependent upon special divine
aid, philosophy and faith, philosophy and theology, are quite
distinct. Certainly with respect to philosophy we would consider it an unwarranted transgression of genera if an argument revealed itself to be essentially dependent for its
cogency and acceptance on an item of faith. On this basis,
the phrase Christian philosophy could be given rather short
shrift. It is on a par, we might want to say, with such phrases

as American philosophy, Irish philosophy, even male philosophy. The connection in the phrase is purely adventitious. It happens that certain arguments and theories have been propounded by Americans or Irishmen or males and this undeniable historical fact has nothing whatever to do with the content of what is maintained, if it is forceful, if it is true. Of course, if it is not true, we may, if we are so inclined, look into the fact that an American said it to see if that provides extenuating circumstances. Finally, I think we want to say that, even if an argument has been formulated by an American, even if we think being an American disposes one to become interested in the area of the argument, one need not be an American to assess the argument, to accept it as true, or reject it as false. When argument is successful, in other words, we can pretty safely ignore the accidental characteristics of its originator.

There have been some who were willing to handle the problem of Christian philosophy in just this way. There are philosophical arguments, tenets, and truths which happen to have been hit upon in a Christian milieu by Christians but precisely to the degree that the arguments are cogent, the tenets tenable, and the truths evidently such, we need make no allusion to the social milieu or to the religious beliefs of their proponents. I don't think the matter is quite that simple but I want to proceed for the moment as if this were unequivocally true. What I would be conceding then is that, from the point of view of content, philosophy is uninfluenced by faith, that what is known is simply different from what is believed. Nevertheless, appeal could here be made to our earlier distinction between philosophy and philosophizing and the question put this way: is religious faith accidental to the philosophizing of the believer?

The Christian Philosopher

What I want to do is to transpose the problem of Christian philosophy to the level where we would rather speak of the Christian philosopher. Being a Christian should surely have a discernible effect on our philosophizing, if only because, as St. Paul put it, our minds have been rendered captive by faith. But in that captivity we are put in possession of the truth that frees so we are at the least rather equivocal bondsmen. Faith may perhaps be described as an intellectual attitude whereby, under the influence of our will, moved by grace, we accept as true what we do not and cannot understand. So described, faith is a possession of the believer; we also speak of *the* faith, what is believed, the object of belief. Ultimately this is someone, God, but it is also what God has told us. God has told us much about himself and about the relation of the world and man to himself, and the believer accepts all these things because God has revealed them—"the whole bag of tricks," as a Graham Greene character not irreverently put it. That is the formality under which he accepts them, God's word; that is why he cannot pick and choose among the things presented for his acceptance. Such picking and choosing is what defines the heretic who is, etymologically, choosy. But on what basis does he choose? On some basis other than the authority of God; perhaps he looks for what is more agreeable to him, less embarrassing, not so far-out. Strictly speaking, such a man does not have faith in the strong sense if faith in the strong sense is accepting on God's word.

Faith is in some sense always and essentially blind if it is the acceptance of things unseen. Nevertheless, because faith is a disposition of mind and it is thanks to mind that we are inquiring beings, questioning beings, the believer soon senses that his mind is an arena of apparently incompatible attitudes. He accepts without question and yet, because he is the kind of being God has made him, he must inquire into and reflect on what he believes. His becomes a faith seeking understanding, a *fides quaerens intellectum*. The presence of inquiry and questioning within a firm adherence to what God has revealed is the source, Aquinas says, of theology.[22] Perhaps we ought not too quickly think of theology as an academic discipline, a kind of learned prowess; Aquinas saw it in continuity with the meditation, the contemplation of the spiritual life. For him, theology was not something undertaken during a kind of recess from the spiritual life; it was, or should be, an expression of the spiritual life. The fruit of the believer's effort to plumb the object of his faith, to draw nearer to it with his whole being, mind, and heart. I think it is fair to say that for Aquinas, theology as he engaged in it, was one mode of the spiritual life. Progress in the spiritual life is not merely a function of our natural capacities and to be a theologian requires a good deal of natural talent. Some of the greatest saints were without learning in any formal sense, but they had the *scientia crucis*, the knowledge of the cross, a lived knowledge which was almost wholly a gift. Surely the ideal would be the person who had both the learning of the theologian and contemplative gifts. St. Thomas was such a one and this fact is not without importance when we try to assess the role the Church has assigned him.[23]

So far, what we have said is that the Christian will feel a natural impulse to inquire into his faith and that this can issue, given a certain natural talent and learning, in what is called theology. A loose but defensible description of theology is the following. Theology is an intellectual effort undertaken by believers and for other believers to put revealed truths into relation with what man can know apart from revelation. By believers, because only they could feel the sustained impulse to undertake the inquiry, only they accept as true the principles of the inquiry; it is for believers, because the function of theology is not to provide faith to those who do not have it or to prove that, given such and such a naturally known truth, a believed truth follows necessarily. Faith is the presupposition of theology, not its effect. If the theologian appears to address every man, this is because he knows that in revelation God speaks to us all and not merely to those who have already received the grace, the ears to hear. Reading theology may be the occasion God uses to give someone faith but then God can employ just about any event or activity as an occasion for granting this gift. It is not the function of theology to create belief; no man can give faith to another, and theology is a human product.

I have gone into this matter at some length—though it is its sinful brevity that bothers me—in order to have a contrast for philosophy. Theology is not philosophy, not because theology is an activity of believers and philosophy is not, but because of the difference in the intrinsic assumptions of the two disciplines. A theological argument presupposes faith because only faith gives the nexus between the components of believed statements. No philosophical argument can be intrinsically reliant on a statement held on faith, whether this be human or divine faith. If a philosophical argument proves anything, this can be seen, in principle, by any man whether or not he has religious faith. What we demand of philosophy, of knowledge, of science, is evidence and cogency. This does not of course require that every philosophical or scientific argument be necessarily conclusive. Perhaps the bulk of our arguments are at best probable, but that probability should be read in terms of the things we are speaking of; it is by appeal to those objects that the force of the argument, whatever its degree, must be read.

If we now ask whether the Christian can devise philosophical or scientific arguments, the quickest way to get an answer would be to find objects of knowledge about which nothing specific has been revealed. Here the Christian will be in the same condition as any man; if he gains reasonable convictions with respect to those objects he must be prepared to sustain them by appeal to what anyone can know about those objects. The mathematics, physics, or logic of the Christian should be indistinguishable from that of the non-Christian and from that of the pagan. Where the problem seems to arise is in areas where the objects under consideration are ones about which the Christian already believes something. Consider the questions mentioned earlier, those bearing on the immortality of the soul and the existence of God. If by Christian philosophy we meant a body of purported knowledge among whose items would be proofs of the soul's immortality and of God's existence which could be cogent only for Christians, by appeal to their faith, then the concept of Christian philosophy is ambiguous at best and ridiculous at worst. Such arguments would not be philosophical in the sense the term had for the most eminent Christian philosopher, St. Thomas Aquinas. No, we must say that if a Christian devises arguments for God's existence or the immortality of the soul, those arguments are philosophical precisely insofar as they are cogent for any man who inspects the evidence provided; there can be no intrinsic dependence on faith in a philosophical argument.

When one consults the literature on Christian philosophy, he finds that no one understands the phrase in the sense of it we have just dismissed as ambiguous and/or ridiculous.[24] Perhaps the note most commonly struck in that literature could be put as follows. Being a Christian gives one a disposition which is not without its effect on the philosophical arguments he devises. That is, Christian philosophy is generally regarded as a matter of Christian philosophizing. This can mean many different things. Two mathematicians are at work at separate blackboards, chalking furiously away. A third mathematician enters, scans the boards, and passes a mathematical judgment on the results of their efforts. One of the two working mathematicians is a Christian and, prior to going to work, he has commended his efforts to God, offered up what he is about to do for the glory of God. The other working mathematician is simply areligious; God and all that sort of thing simply do not engage his attention. When he set to work he resolved to do his damnedest to come up with something that would knock the third mathematician—the chairman of the department, as it happens— off his gouty feet. The point is that the motive of the Christian mathematician is decidedly different, but we do not expect him to get extra credit in mathematics for it. Nonetheless, when we recall our earlier discussions of morality and the intellectual life, we could come up with some kind of argument to the effect that the Christian attitude may, in one possessing the requisite talent, provide motives which would have salutary effects within mathematics. If he is a good Christian and not motivated by pride or vanity, he is thereby free of possible impediments to doing mathematics well. But of course one need not be a Christian to be free of those impediments. Since we have reached this far for a favorable concomitant of belief, we must also mention that the Christian attitude could favor sloppy mathematics. The Christian might think a passion for correctness or creativity were inimical to his ultimate destiny and perform accordingly. Perhaps we would want to dismiss this second example as a misunderstanding, but if we appeal to the concrete we must allow for the effects of faith as it is found in the believers who are.

There is really little point in pursuing such considerations. They are inevitably forced and, more crucially, they connect only minimally with the questions discussed when the matter of Christian philosophy comes up. This is not to say that the move from philosophy to philosophizing is not appropriate here, but that we do not yet have in hand the information that makes the move important and interesting.

Let us go back to what we said earlier about revelation and faith. In speaking of these, we gave the impression that the sum total of what has been revealed must be believed in the strong sense precisely because it is beyond man's ken in this life. This must now be qualified. As it happens, a goodly amount has been revealed which men can in principle know apart from revelation. This is the area of what Aquinas called the *praeambula fidei*, preambles of faith. For example, to accept revelation is to accept the existence of God but it is also to accept as true that men can apart from revelation know that God exists.[25] To accept revelation is to accept that man's destiny transcends the fact of death, that his goal is eternal happiness with God. Many Christians, nevertheless, feel, with some other philosophers, that by natural reason alone we can arrive at knowledge of the immortality of the soul. One of the more striking aspects of revelation is that it contains what came to be called natural law precepts. Now a natural law precept is a moral norm that one cannot fail to see by reflecting on the human situation, on the kind of agent man is. Why would God in revelation speak to man of things man knows, or could come to know, apart from revelation?[26]

From a Christian point of view, this oddity is rather easily explained. It is one thing to speak of philosophy and the intrinsic demands and character of philosophy; it is quite another matter when we consider the men who engage in philosophizing. For the Christian, man is in a fallen condition, he bears on his soul the marks of the fall of the race in Adam. The net effect of this is that man, however clear we may be as to his destiny naturally considered, that is, apart from grace and faith, is in a condition where it is highly unlikely that he will perform even his natural activities well. As a result of sin, original and personal, man's mind is darkened, his nature disordered, his appetites at war with reason. In the moral order he often fails to recognize even common norms of behavior, norms which are anchored precisely in the kind of agent he is. His culture reflects his behavior and the young are raised in ways which can systematically prevent them from seeing the way things are. In a nutshell, to the Christian, it becomes painfully obvious that man needs grace, needs the supernatural, in order to do correctly or well what he is naturally inclined to do. That is, in order to be a good man one must have the aid of grace. Notice that what is being said is not simply that grace is necessary to man if he is to achieve his supernatural goal; it is necessary for him if he is to achieve his natural goal. "Necessary" varies in meaning in those two claims; grace is absolutely necessary in the first instance, more likely than not, by and large, necessary in the second.

The effect of such considerations, which, as stated, commend themselves only to the believer, on philosophy is remarkable. If natural reasoning must begin with evident truths and if, for one reason or another, a man can fail to accept even the evident, the Christian whose faith englobes those truths has an extra-philosophical ground for being disposed to see them. His faith provides him with guideposts for his thinking, navigational stars that are fixed both in the evidence of things and in his faith. Furthermore, if he believes that God exists, if he believes the soul is immortal, if he believes there are naturally knowable norms for human action, he is disposed to ground these in evidence other than revelation. Notice that his faith does not provide him with philosophical arguments; it does provide him with convictions and certitudes about things that can be known and his conviction and certitude are antecedent to his knowledge, if he goes on to acquire it. Of course the non-believer would be incensed by such talk and I am under no illusion that what I am saying could be cogent for him. What I am trying to describe is the attitude of the Christian as he engages in philosophy. The non-believer can be rightly without interest in that antecedent certitude; he will and should demand from the Christian philosopher arguments which are independent of his extra-philosophical certitudes. Nevertheless, for the Christian philosopher, the conviction and certitude he has from his faith are a tremendous boon when he philosophizes. He may search twenty years and more for a cogent proof of God's existence and know he has not found it. Yet, while he will continue to strive to find that proof, while he retains all kinds of extra-philosophical motives for continuing the search, he does not doubt that God exists. His doubt doesn't bear on his attempted proofs; he *knows* the ones he has so far come up with are no good. But he knows, thanks to his faith, that God exists. Would he, if he proved, really proved, God's existence, continue to believe? Yes, he would, because God as he can be known and God as he is believed in by the Christian are one God seen under different aspects. It is sometimes said that a proved God is no God. By that is meant, I suspect, that no philosophical proof could ever ground the total commitment that is the Christian life, and that is true. But Christians must believe that God can be known by non-Christians, by pagans. When St. Paul spoke of the Romans, he was not saying that they had rejected faith; he was saying that they knew God exists and failed to live accordingly and thereby fell into the vices he goes on to record. The God some pagans knew and the God Christians believe is the same God; the God whose existence I might prove and the God whom I believe and would continue to believe are the same God. But what I can *know* of God and what I *believe* of God are different and will remain different. That is why the oft-repeated remark that the God of Aristotle and the God of revelation are different does not have the import it is thought to have. The remark, in context, suggests that there is something incompatible between what philosophers say of God and what Christians believe of God; this may be true, but it is not necessarily true, true by the nature of the case. What is true by the nature of the case is that philosophers will never know about God what can only be believed of him, but of course that recognition does not lead us to chide the philosopher.

The phrase Christian philosophy can be made to deliver up this sense. Thanks to their faith, Christians are in possession of certitude about a number of crucial truths which can be known apart from faith; their antecedent certitude sustains their quest even though it does not as such provide them with the arguments on which natural knowledge of the truths in question may depend. Because faith embraces two regions, what can be known as well as what cannot be known but only believed, he cannot accept the possibility that something would be conclusively true for reason which is in conflict with what he believes. He knows, with the certitude of faith, that no one could conclusively show that it is impossible that God exists. This conviction does not provide him with a philosophical refutation, of course, but it prods him to find one. Quite apart from its influence in areas of conflict between reason and faith, the Christian attitude is a powerful motive for seeking knowledge. If knowledge is a perfection of our nature, if grace builds on nature, then the fullness of being to which he is called will include as much knowledge as he can acquire. Rather than being an invitation to obscurantism, faith should be a felt obligation to intellectual inquiry.

The ringing rhetoric of those final claims may sound a leaden echo in the secular mind. How can one who admits that for the Christian there are extra-philosophical guideposts to reasoning, antecedent certitudes that await sustaining arguments, possibly speak of free inquiry and withstand the charge of obscurantism? It would be possible to reply to this by saying that no one really is prepared to follow an argument to whatever term. For example, if someone undertakes to prove to the physicist that the physical world is not really there to be studied, few physicists will be apt to listen with an open mind. They have prejudged the issue. They have not the least doubt in the reality of the external world. If they listen, they look for flaws, for leaps, for ambiguities and, when they find them, they sense with joy that their antecedent conviction is being indirectly confirmed. There is a sense of free inquiry such that free inquiry is not even an abstract possibility for men—where free means unencumbered by any certitudes prior to a given argument. There is no argument which does not assume something and assume it as certain; that is, take it to be certain as opposed to seeing what it would be like if. Of course faith may be an impediment to knowledge; throughout the history of Christianity there has been a running battle between the dialecticians and the anti-dialecticians. But faith need not be an impediment, it does not prevent one from being a philosopher; it can and should be a stimulus to do philosophy.

Concluding Summary

Since in the course of this chapter we gave an interim summary of the argument, we can be brief here. Beginning with a disgruntled Catholic who wondered about the intellectual respectability of a philosophy curriculum influenced by the wishes of the Church, we sought to allay his fears by pointing out that any beginning student of philosophy is placed in a position where he has to trust the framers of a curriculum. Talk about a trust or belief antecedent to knowledge led us into a discussion of the influence of the extra-philosophical on philosophical knowing, and we introduced the distinction between philosophy and philosophizing and, in terms of the latter, sought to show why once upon a time the influence of moral dispositions on thinking was a problem directly faced. That we still retain an inclination to recognize the importance of moral attitudes in the intellectual life was shown in a number of ways. The hope was that, with all this as background, a discussion of the influence of religious faith on philosophy could be undertaken in such a way that it would not appear a wholly unusual state of affairs. The problem of Christian philosophy was addressed in terms of the Christian philosopher, the philosophizing the Christian engages in, and we hoped to show that this involves nothing inimical to philosophy as such but rather a possibly beneficial influence on philosophy. At the least we hoped to show that the believer can be a philosopher. If this has been established, we are prepared to undertake a discussion of the specific advice the Church has given the Catholic concerning the study of philosophy, namely, *Ite ad Thomam:* Go to Thomas.

NOTES

1. For Aquinas on faith, see *Summa theologiae*, IIaIIae, qq. 1–7; *Q.D. de veritate*, q. 14.

2. Josef Pieper, *Belief and Faith, A Philosophical Tract*, New York, 1963.

3. For Aristotle on the influence of the familiar on inquiry, see *Metaphysics*, II, 3.

4. "It makes no small difference, then, whether we form habits of one kind or of another from our very youth; it makes a very great difference, or rather *all* the difference." *Nicomachean Ethics*, II, 1.

5. See Aquinas, *Q.D. de veritate*, q. 2, a. 2.

6. For this conception of the nature of logic, see my *The Logic of Analogy*, Martinus Nijhoff, The Hague, 1961.

7. See J. Pieper, *Leisure the Basis of Culture*, Mentor-Omega Edition, New York, 1963, pp. 69 ff.

8. See "Kierkegaard and Speculative Thought" in *The New Scholasticism*, January, 1966.

9. What I am getting at here may be tied up with Husserl's notion of the *lebenswelt*. See James Collins, "Husserl and the Bond of Natural Being," in *Three Paths of Philosophy*, pp. 348 ff.

10. "The real subject is not the cognitive subject, since in knowing he moves in the sphere of the possible; the real subject is the ethically existing subject." *Kierkegaard's Concluding Unscientific Postscript*, tr. Swenson and Lowrie, Princeton, 1944, p. 281.

11. See Charles DeKoninck's introduction in S. Cantin, *Précis de psychologie thomiste*, Quebec, 1948, pp. vii-lxxxiii and DeKoninck's *The Hollow Universe*, New York, 1961.

12. *Nicomachean Ethics*, I, 7.

13. Unamuno, *The Tragic Sense of Life*, Dover Edition, New York, 1954.

14. "But as more arts were invented, and some were directed to the necessities of life, others to recreation, the inventors of the latter were naturally always regarded as wiser than the inventors of the former, because their branches of knowledge did not aim at util-

ity. Hence when all such inventions were already established, the sciences which do not aim at giving pleasure or at the necessities of life were discovered, and first in the places where men first began to have leisure." *Metaphysics*, I, 1. In the next chapter, Aristotle puts the point in a single sentence. "All the sciences, indeed, are more necessary than this, but none is better."

15. An important exception is Max Scheler. See his *On the Eternal in Man*, London, 1960.

16. *IIaIIae*, q. 49, a. 3, ad 1m.

17. *Ibid.*, q. 53, a. 3.

18. *IIaIIae*, q. 166, a. 2.

19. On all this, see T. MacLellan, "The Moral Virtues and the Speculative Life," *Laval théologique et philosophique*, XII, 2 (1956), pp. 175–232.

20. See note 1 above and Pieper's *Belief and Faith*.

21. See the *Postscript*, p. 189.

22. *Q.D. de veritate*, q. 14, a. 1, ad 5m.

23. Maritain has always insisted on the continuity of the intellectual and spiritual lives, an insistence built into the title of his masterpiece, *Les degres du savoir*.

24. The following books are among those I have in mind when I speak of the literature on Christian philosophy. E. Gilson, *Christianity and Philosophy*, New York, 1939; J. V. Langmead-Casserly, *The Christian in Philosophy*, London, 1949; Luigi Bogliolo, *Il Problema della Filosofia Cristiana*, Brescia, 1959; Fidel G. Martinez, *De l'authenticité d'une philosophie à l'intérieur de la pensée chrétienne*, Oña, n.d.; R. Jolivet, *La philosophie chrétienne et la pensée contemporaine*, Paris, 1932; M. Nedoncelle, *Existe-t-il une philosophie chrétienne?* Paris, 1956; A. C. Pegis, *Christian Philosophy and Intellectual Freedom*, Milwaukee, 1955; A. Naud, *Le problème de la philosophie chrétienne*, Montreal, 1960.

25. For the notion of preambles of faith, see *Summa theologiae*, Ia, q. 1, a. 2, ad 1m. That God's existence can be known apart from faith was taught by Vatican I as the clear sense of *Romans*, I, 20.

26. See Josef Fuchs, *Natural Law*, New York, 1965.

CHAPTER FOUR

THE ROLE OF ST. THOMAS

In order to talk about the role St. Thomas can continue to play in our intellectual life, it is necessary first of all to talk about encompassing issues. That is what we tried to do in the preceding chapters. Some expressions of discontent with the fact of Thomism actually have a far broader target for they call into question the inevitable consequences of being taught philosophy, of learning philosophy. To the degree that one learns philosophy he is brought into relation with a tradition, he accepts on extra-philosophical grounds a curriculum, a course, and a teacher. This is not the unique plight of the Catholic in a given kind of school; it is a common situation and one which has advantages as well as disadvantages. As soon as this point is made, its obviousness is unmistakable; yet it has been overlooked and its being overlooked has led to weird and unreal criticisms; its being recalled can bring us gently back to the real world where we can confront the genuine difficulties of present-day Thomism.

If the Catholic shares with any beginning student of philosophy the need to trust, to accept, to suspend disbelief, there is a feature of his philosophizing which is less generic and that stems precisely from the fact that he has faith. Some Catholics have expressed embarrassment at the suggestion that they differ in any way from their fellow philosophers because they possess the gift of faith. The exact nature of the influence of faith on our philosophy is difficult to determine; nevertheless, it is or should be real, its influence can be seen as beneficial and beneficial philosophically. To be a Catholic is, after all, to hold rather determinate views on the present condition of man, his ability to achieve his natural end apart from the help of grace, and all this, we suggested, has its importance for discussions of how man can pursue successfully his natural impulse to know. Faith makes foolish the wisdom of this world, but surely that does not mean there is no wisdom apart from revelation; knowledge becomes foolish when it is mistakenly regarded as inimical to what God has revealed, when it becomes an impediment to faith. It is foolish, not because it refuses to be put to some extrinsic use; it is foolish because it fails to meet the intrinsic criteria of knowledge. The Catholic has an antecedent certitude that no valid knowledge can be inimical to what has been revealed by God. His faith is therefore a kind of measure of his philosophy; his faith gives him confidence and comfort when the going gets rough. What is here being recalled is what the believer holds, not what anyone, believer or not, must recognize to be the case. The only adequate philosophical test of these convictions will be in philosophical positions and arguments which commend themselves to believer and non-believer alike. To recall this extra-philosophical influence, which the believer holds will have a salutary effect within philosophy, should not be embarrassing for the Catholic. If he is embarrassed by such reminders, surely he should examine the phenomenon of embarrassment and see what its sources and justification might be. It is a melancholy fact of the history of philosophy that extra-philosophical influences other than faith explain odd jumps, lacunae, and a systematic indifference to certain issues; in any philosopher there are tenets and favored topics which cannot be explained within philosophy. Why does Heidegger simply refuse to let God intrude into his philosophy? One who inspects his chosen area of study without Heidegger's resolve to keep the ontology finite will have difficulty discerning in the things spoken about any warrant for this restriction. Why does Sartre simply assert that God cannot exist? Why did some philosophers insist that religious and ethical statements are devoid of meaning? Once one makes such options he can construct a theory which seems to favor them, but the resulting theory soon reveals itself to be in such flagrant contradiction with what we knew and knew for certain before undertaking the formal study of philosophy that a following generation has to dethrone the controlling assumption and admit as meaningful what no one ever seriously considered to be meaningless. My point is that every philosopher is influenced in his philosophizing and resultant theory by antecedent attitudes. The Christian is no different generically but when he turns to the specific influence of his faith, can he regard it as arbitrary, as a menace, as without justifiable import for philosophy? Just as faith is reasonable, so the influence of faith on philosophy is reasonable. The same cannot be said for every antecedent influence on philosophizing. Many Catholics attempt to by-pass such considerations by carefully selecting areas of study where the meeting of knowledge and faith is minimal or non-existent. I have sometimes thought that formal logic attracts for this reason, were this so, one might say, varying a title of A. N. Prior, escapism is the ethical verdict on logic. Analytic philosophy regarded as a technique without philosophical content could exercise a similar attraction. What happens then is that one avoids the big questions which have always been definitive of philosophy because, of course, those big questions will always raise, at least for discussions of philosophical activity, of philosophizing, the further question of the relation of this activity to one's religious faith. When an interest in logic or analysis is not merely an expression of the division of intellectual labor, but of a systematic turning away from the broad and big questions, the result is not merely a personal confusion which can reach a high emotional pitch, but also a denaturing of philosophy itself.

Like all students of philosophy, the Catholic is under the influence of what can be called tradition; unlike many other students of philosophy, the Catholic is under the influence of his faith—though, again, this does not mean that the other students of philosophy are without antecedent influences. The difference is that it is quite easy for the Catholic to isolate and describe this principal influence on his intellectual inquiries and to go on to see its desirability and advantages of a more or less a priori sort. The proof of the value of faith as an antecedent influence must be read in its consequences: philosophical positions assessable in terms of the intrinsic criteria of philosophy. Antecedent influences other than faith are also present in the Catholic philosopher, of course, but they are more amorphous, less easy to isolate and describe.

Now what interests us here is not simply the fact that our faith influences our philosophy, but the really quite extraordinary fact that the Church has again and again and over many centuries explicitly recommended St. Thomas Aquinas to the faithful as their primary preceptor in philosophy.

The Authority of St. Thomas

It would be possible to draw up an impressive list of ecclesiastical documents bearing on the study of Thomas Aquinas, but it is not necessary to do so. Father Ramirez has already done it in as thorough a fashion as one could wish.[1] No one can doubt that the Church, through the ordinary magisterium, which is of course fallible, has again and again and in quite unmistakable terms recommended to Catholics as a sure guide in philosophy, as their first teacher in this area, St. Thomas Aquinas. It is the meaning and import of this fact that has caused difficulty, which continues to cause difficulty, and about which opinions are severely divided. A correct understanding of what the Church is doing here is of an extreme importance lest some use these documents as an occasion to excoriate their fellows, question their sincerity and faith, or seek to settle philosophical differences by a citation from an encyclical or a papal allocution. A proper understanding of these documents is no less necessary to forestall any likening of the recommendation of Aquinas to the condemnation of Galileo, or regarding the repeated recommendation by the ordinary magisterium as a welcome occasion to exhibit one's indifference to, or liberty in the face of, such dark Italianate crypto-fascism said to have nothing to do with the Christian faith. These documents, let it be said, should be neither an invitation to release the latent Torquemada in every breast nor an occasion for juvenile protestations of disregard for those conservatives in Rome. A tradition of the longevity of this one can hardly be lightly dismissed by a serious Catholic. I should think that each of us, certainly those of us who are professionally engaged in philosophy, owes it to himself to reflect on the meaning of this tradition and meditate on its significance for his own philosophizing. Ten years ago this would have been a superfluous suggestion; I rather doubt there were many Catholic philosophers then who had not arrived at a reflective position on the question. Today is a different matter altogether, I think. For many reasons, some of them examined by Professor James Collins,[2] there is an increasing number of young Catholics who have finished or are finishing their graduate work in philosophy, often in non-Catholic schools, who will be joining the philoso-

phy staffs of Catholic colleges. The situation before us is
one of immense opportunity, consequently, but as well one of
great potential danger. Unless we recognize the situation and
respond intelligently to it, it is not impossible that there could
be repeated in Catholic institutions the kind of philosophical
chaos that obtained when Leo XIII issued *Aeterni patris*. On
the other hand, the situation could be likened, *mutatis mutandis*, to that which confronted Aquinas himself, and surely
those of us who lay claim to the title of Thomist would be
far less than we should be if we could not reflect in our efforts something of the open, eager, even delighted responsive-
ness with which Thomas regarded an intellectual era in a state
of rapid and sometimes confusing flux.

I hope that our earlier considerations have made it clear
that there is nothing in itself unusual about the Catholic's receiving advice at the outset of his study of philosophy. If our
earlier point was made, we will be in agreement that anyone
who begins the formal study of philosophy is under a comparable influence. But if any novice in philosophy must trust
for a time his elders, the situation to which we are making
reference seems decidedly different. The faith involved would
seem to be not simply human faith, but religious faith. Let
us be as clear as possible here, in order that a grievous misunderstanding can be avoided. The Catholic is not asked to
believe St. Thomas Aquinas in the strong sense of believe;
there is no suggestion here that anything Aquinas might
have taught or written could, just as such, be considered as
part of the deposit of faith the Catholic must believe. No
Catholic does, or is called upon to, believe a philosophy or a
theology. Our effort to distinguish between faith and reason,
philosophy and theology, should make this clear. No philosophical position or argument is, as such, *de fide;* there is
only one way to sustain a position philosophically and that is
by argument, by appeal to the relevant evidence, by the co-

gency with which one reasons, and this must all be such that the appeal is to any mind, whether Christian or not. Nothing the Church has said about the study of Aquinas conflicts or could conflict with that basic truth which has to do with the integrity of human reason. The recommendation of Aquinas bears on our initiation to philosophy and the Church speaks here not simply out of the generic concern that one man or group of men might have for the younger generation. The Church is not simply Uncle George. As a divine agency, she has as her role the guarding and teaching of the deposit of faith. It is that proper concern which has led the Church to speak as well of philosophical instruction, not because philosophical instruction is part of the deposit of faith, but rather because many philosophical discussions impinge on the deposit of faith which is in the custody of the Church. The Church, then, is addressing the activity we have called philosophizing, the area where our subjective dispositions are essentially involved. The distinction between philosophy and faith, considered in themselves, abstractly, is neat and clear; the connection between philosophizing and faith is, in the believer, I should think, inevitable. His faith, bearing as it does on the Church in her proper role, will affect his disposition with respect to the ordinary magisterium of the Church. The livelier his faith, the more disposed he will be to take into account what that ordinary magisterium has to say. In reflecting on what the Church has to say about philosophical instruction, he can come to see the reasonableness of such advice. One who has devoted some years to philosophy can easily see that some modes of initiation to philosophy could involve distinct and unnecessary dangers to faith. What more reasonable then than that the agency which has been entrusted with the task of guarding the deposit of faith should speak out on this matter? As the Fathers of Vatican II put it: "To fulfill the mandate she has received from her divine

founder of proclaiming the mystery of salvation to all men
and of restoring all things in Christ, Holy Mother the Church
must be concerned with the whole of man's life, even the
secular part of it insofar as it has a bearing on his heavenly
calling."[3] What reason could a Catholic have for rejecting
out of hand such advice of the Church? Surely it would be
difficult to sustain the opinion that the Church has no business
to speak out in this area; surely one would be wanting in
docility if, while conceding the Church's right, he chose simply to ignore it. Moreover, a philosopher who rejects an
Aquinas he has not read can scarcely be thought of as passing a philosophical judgment. Quite apart from the expressed
wishes of the Church, a Catholic philosopher who rejected
Aquinas as irrelevant for our times has at the very least the
burden of proof. I have little doubt that one could draw
up a list of passages and positions from Aquinas which could
be shown, on a philosophical basis, to be inadequate, unlikely,
and even false. On that basis, their irrelevance would follow as a matter of course. Were someone to draw up such a
syllabus of errors and establish their falsehood, inadequacy,
or unlikelihood, no one could fail to take seriously such an
effort. But this would be *toto coelo* different from the claim,
made by one who had not seriously examined Aquinas, that
his thought is irrelevant to the twentieth century. This is not
the expression of a judgment, but of an antecedent attitude
and one I should find surprising in a Catholic.

Aquinas as Symbol

If the Church has the right, given her proper task, to speak
out on the matter of philosophical instruction and if the
Catholic who is well disposed can be expected to take into

account what the Church teaches, even when this is a matter of the ordinary magisterium, there arises the question as to the continuing status of the substantive doctrine of the Aquinas the Church recommends in a special way. However, I would like, first of all, to suggest a minimal way in which Aquinas could always continue to function as a guide for the Catholic philosopher. In the Decree on Christian Education, promulgated at Vatican II, we read the following. "In those schools dependent on her, she [the Church] intends that by their very constitution individual subjects be pursued according to their own principles, method and inquiry, in such a way that an ever deeper understanding in these fields will be obtained and that, as questions that are new and current are raised and investigations made according to the example of the doctors of the Church and especially of St. Thomas Aquinas, there may be a deeper realization of the harmony of faith and science."[4] We notice that Aquinas is here mentioned by name but that he functions as a kind of symbol of the intellectual activity of the Catholic. What he is symbolic of is the concern the Catholic intellectual will have to relate what he knows from his study of the various sciences to what he believes. The present pope has sounded a number of warnings against fideism, against the tendency to dissociate reason and faith. "Your studies can also help to dispel the error of some believers who are currently tempted by a renewed fideism. By trusting scientific thought alone and distrusting the certitude proper to philosophical wisdom, they are forced to base their adherence to truths of a metaphysical order on a decision of the will. In face of this abdication of the intelligence, which tends to destroy the traditional doctrine on the preambles of faith, your work must again call attention to the irreplaceable value of natural reason, solemnly declared by Vatican Council I in conformity with the constant teaching of the Church, one of whose most authoritative and outstanding witnesses is Saint Thomas Aquinas."[5] Once more Aquinas is cited as an example, as a symbol, of a certain kind of Christian concern. If the Christian must endeavor to relate everything in his life to his calling, we are faced here with a particularization of that general task. The intellectual, the scientist, the philosopher, must as Christians see their work in the light of their faith. This does not simply mean that they direct their efforts, as human acts, to their supernatural goal, but also that they meditate on the significance of what they come to know for what they believe. Paul VI refers to the traditional doctrine on the preambles of faith, something we touched on earlier. The Catholic is held to believe that God can be known by natural reason apart from revelation; even if some things which can be naturally known have *de facto* been revealed, these can be distinguished from what has been revealed and cannot be understood by natural reason. Thus, the non-believer as well as the believer can come to know on a basis other than faith truths about the same God concerning whom the Christian believes yet other truths. It is because God can be the object both of faith and of natural reason that there is a kind of bridge between the two; not again that faith can be deduced from reason, not that acceptance of a proof of God's existence makes one a Christian. But if one knows God exists, on the basis of natural reason, he may be disposed to hear what God has revealed to man. For the believer, such natural proofs of God's existence are a powerful adjunct; God can no longer seem an object gained by a voluntaristic leap in the dark. Furthermore, when the Christian philosopher sees the limits and poverty of natural knowledge of God, he will be disposed to be grateful for what God in his goodness has told us of himself. Is this to say that the faith of the philosopher differs from that of the simple man because he is a philosopher? Not on the point I have mentioned, certainly, since the simple man too must accept as defined that man can naturally come to know that God exists. Whatever the limitations of his personal talents, the simple believer cannot hold that faith is man's only access to the existence of God. In short, it is the belief of Catholics that faith and natural reason cannot be opposed in such a way that the former alone can attain to God and the latter has simply a finite range of objects, knowledge of which has no relation whatsoever to knowledge of God. I take the pope's warning against fideism to be a reminder to us, particularly to intellectuals, of what we do in fact believe. I take him to be warning against regarding science and/or philosophy as neutral or irrelevant to what we believe. He tells us that we cannot seriously hold this and he points out a long tradition of attempts on the part of Christian thinkers to bring into relationship with one another the fruits of natural knowledge and the truths of faith. The symbol of that effort is St. Thomas Aquinas. If then the pope is mentioning a task more or less incumbent on every Catholic engaged in the various pursuits of the intellectual life, and if Thomas Aquinas is the privileged symbol of that task, then the Christian intellectual is, to that degree, called to be a Thomist. That is, called to do the sort of thing Thomas did or tried to do.

What I have just described was earlier billed as a minimal response to the Church's wishes. It goes without saying that Thomism means a great deal more than this acceptance of a generic task, both to Thomists and their opponents. It means a good deal more than this to me. But, without being excessively irenic, I wanted to devise a meaning for the term Thomist which would be broad enough to cover an essential obligation of the Christian intellectual (if I read the pope correctly). This is what I had in mind when, in my first chapter, I said that there is no real alternative to Thomism open to the Catholic philosopher. He should be about the kind of business Aquinas was about as a philosopher. That at least any Catholic philosopher can accept from the Church's recommendations. One might wonder why we couldn't as easily say that any Catholic philosopher must be an Augustinian or Bonaventurian or Boethian. On the level of the minimal response, there is no reason why we couldn't have used those designations—except that the Church, when she singles out a Christian thinker to symbolize the task, has a penchant for Aquinas. Perhaps one reason for this is that to symbolize the common task as Thomist is to leave out so very little that would be connoted by the other adjectives and to imply a good deal more, at least with respect to the quality and scope of the effort. A Thomist who is not a student of Augustine, of Boethius, of Denys the Areopagite, of Abelard, Erigena, the Victorines—one could go on and on—what would a Thomist without those interests be? But that is to get into the more substantive interpretation of Thomism, and there is a discussion we must undertake as a preliminary to that.

Past Responses to Aquinas

When we were speaking of the difference between the Catholic and the non-Catholic with regard to the status of the one giving advice on where to begin the study of philosophy, we made the point that the Catholic must regard himself as being in a more favorable position. The advice he is following emanates from a source he simply cannot think of as on the same level as a merely human agency. He will have, we suggested, a far greater antecedent assurance that he is setting out on the right path. Uncle George could be wrong, even *Time* could be wrong, but the Catholic is unlikely to think that the Church can be wrong on a matter on which she has spoken so consistently and over so long a period of time. Having said that, we added that matters are not really so simple and radiant for the Catholic. I am sure the reader surmised my meaning, but I will nonetheless develop it; it would be rather late in this essay to refrain from laboring the obvious.

Mediating between the Catholic enrolling for his first philosophy course and the advice of the Church that he begin with St. Thomas are at least two things: the curriculum of the school and the particular instructor he has drawn in the mad lottery called registration. The curriculum embodies an institutional response to the Church's wishes, and let us imagine that it is a fairly positive kind of response; the curriculum represents an interpretation of those wishes in terms of an undergraduate in an American Catholic college in the twentieth century. Presumably the curriculum contains more than one philosophy course, and our beginner must take several if he is one day to be graduated. Now, as it happens, not every philosophy curriculum in American Catholic colleges is the same; the required courses vary in number and content; where there is a similarity in required courses, the order in which they must or may be taken varies. All this boils down to one response among many to the Church's wishes, a response devised or agreed upon or lived with by a number of individual philosophers. My quite obvious point is that, in the concrete, the young Catholic beginning the study of philosophy is subject to an advice which is every bit as human, all too human, as that to which the student in a non-Catholic college is subject. Beyond the curriculum, there is the individual instructor he chances to get. He may have had no choice in the matter; he may have had a choice and exercised it by seeking advice from other students. Let us imagine that what guided his decision was not the information that Professor Pumpernickel is an easy grader, but the repeated claim that he teaches a good course. Our beginner is once more deeply involved in trusting of a sort not unlike that of a student in a non-Catholic college. Anyway, here now he is, seated with others before the sapiential visage of Professor Pumpernickel. The course about to begin may be regarded by the teacher as Thomistic in orientation but, as we mentioned in the introductory chapter, there are Thomists and Thomists and we can assume that Professor Pumpernickel is of one sort or another. In brief, our novice is not simply beginning the study of philosophy under the guidance of Aquinas; he is being introduced to Aquinas by one of several possible routes. Let us consider some introductions to Aquinas which have not led to a lasting friendship.

The situation in seminaries should be considered first since many of the current critiques of Thomism come from men who took their philosophy in seminaries. Not a million years ago, the situation looked something like this. Philosophy was begun in what corresponded to junior and senior years of college, during which years the seminarian was referred to as a philosopher, a title he may not have claimed nor been accorded since. During those two years, the seminarian took a staggering number of courses in philosophy: logic, epistemology, metaphysics, natural theology, cosmology, psychology, ethics, the history of philosophy. Some of these courses were a semester in length, others two, the history often four semesters in duration. In bleaker houses, the medium of instruction was a textbook, perhaps written in a Latin the quality of which made the seminarian who had gained something from long years of study in the classics wince. One priest told me the only philosophical problem he ever had in the seminary was whether or not he would pass the course. If we can believe the critics, the tone of the course was what can only be called catechetical. Here is the thesis we maintain; here are the grounds for it; here are erroneous options to our thesis. Go and commit it all to memory. Whether or not the text was in Latin, it received a kind of attention and devotion rarely accorded books. How many philosophers have said or written things they would seriously want others to memorize verbatim? We would like to be praised or damned for what we actually said, of course, but the thought of huge paragraphs, even pages, being uncritically committed to memory involves a type of adulation few philosophers would wish. Yet this is the way many manualists were treated, men whose claim to intellectual fame often rested solely on the manual, men unknown to philosophical colleagues, contemporaries of theirs on the wider scene. If there was anything more striking than this demand on the student, it was the self-effacing diffidence of the instructor. It was not unknown for a seminary professor to long publicly for the parish life and wish to be free from the drudgery of teaching. It was not unheard of for a seminary instructor to be unable to elucidate the text the students were poring over. It was not surprising that young men who were subjected to this sort of thing failed to learn. They were not being asked to learn. The manual might as well have been Holy Writ; the point was to get it into one's memory and be able to disgorge it on demand.

This is a pretty bleak picture. I cannot say whether or not it is a true one. Nothing in my own experience matches it and I spent two years of my life being, successively, a First

Philosopher and a Second Philosopher. But many will assure us that they endured some such instruction and, even allowing for dyspepsia and hyperbole, one is forced to conclude that in some seminaries things have been rather less than intellectually exciting.

Even in some fairly good seminaries, there were professors who gave the impression that every meaningful philosophical question had already been framed and a definitive answer to it found. This conviction may not always have vitiated their teaching in any radical way, but it hardly conduced to an attitude of eagerness and inquiry. Even in the better places, however, the range of sources considered pertinent to the discussion of a philosophical question was severely limited. It would have been difficult, perhaps, to find a seminary that would not have claimed to be teaching Thomistic philosophy, but it would have been equally difficult to find one where the students were urged or expected to read Aquinas. The point is that the restriction of the range of sources was not to the texts of Aquinas; rather it was to secondary sources, usually manuals, often Latin manuals. And it seems to have been the rare place that required students to read anything other than the textbook for a given course. This point must be underlined when we consider the phenomenon of anti-Thomism among the clergy. Few of them ever read Thomas Aquinas, apart from a citation in the manual; few of them were really engaged in philosophical inquiry, even in terms of limited sources. Here and there, presumably, a rare seminarian did more than he was required to do; he read primary sources, he read the philosophical journals in the seminary library. But by and large, even good students were led to see the task of philosophy in terms of warring interpretations of medieval texts, of medieval schools.

What of the courses in the history of philosophy? Surely

these would have broadened the philosophical outlook of the seminarian? In some cases, this seems to have happened, though there was always a problem with some original sources and the Index. That was not an insurmountable problem, of course, and the question remains whether seminarians were urged to go beyond the narrative presentation of a philosopher's teachings, laid out in the history of philosophy text, to the man's writings. Even with the inclination, however, the seminarian was so busy with so many courses that it would have been difficult for him to undertake that further reading.

Imagine this situation, paint it blacker or less black, as you will, and then consider the case of the clerical anti-Thomist. If things were as bad as I have attempted to describe them, on the basis of quite audible hearsay, could anyone blame the victim for his discontent? I feel constrained to repeat that this dark picture does not match my memories of my sojourn in the seminary; I feel equally constrained to add how surprised I have been to hear friends from those days who, in their indifference to matters intellectual could have gone unscathed by the instruction of Socrates himself, lament in retrospect the quality of seminary instruction. There is doubtless much exaggeration going on here, but equally doubtless we have to admit that seminary philosophy, as it has been described, invites reaction. And yet, assuming all those depressing tales are true, I would want to insist that to reject *that* can hardly be the same thing as rejecting the philosophy of Thomas Aquinas. I would concede that the rejection is a rejection of Thomism, since that is what this seminary instruction claimed to be. But since, by general report, it involved practically no direct contact with the writings of Aquinas, it is not and should not be described as a rejection of Aquinas. I hope it will be granted that this is no mere nitpicking distinction. To make it is not, of course, to question the correctness of the rejection that is being made. If what is described as the nature of past seminary instruction were Thomism, I would say, Away with Thomism! If the sort of thing one can find in many of the manuals to which reference is made were Thomism, I would say, Away with Thomism! What I do say is away with that sort of Thomism and I will go on to say that that sort of thing is not at all what Leo XIII had in mind when he wrote *Aeterni patris*. Something has intervened between Leo XIII and John XXIII, something in many ways unfortunate. But that is something for a later place.

First we must return to our college freshman. We left him in order to examine the plight of the seminarian. That was not entirely a detour, as it happens, because in the not too distant past the philosophy curriculum of Catholic laymen was modeled, to a greater or lesser degree, on that devised for seminarians. To a certain extent, accordingly, many of the bad aspects of seminary philosophy were carried over into the college offerings. A rash of textbook series appeared and, as with itching and scratching, it seemed for a time that the flood would never cease. At the moment it has been reduced to the merest trickle. What principle lay behind those textbooks? Let me discuss one basis for them, one with which I am acquainted. Philosophy is the name of a class of disciplines which culminate in metaphysics; the purpose of teaching philosophy is to bring students along to metaphysics as the crowning course. As prerequisites for it, logic, philosophy of nature and psychology, at least, must first be studied. All right, what was needed, the assumption ran, were textbooks giving a rounded if capsulized presentation of each of those disciplines. When these disciplines were viewed from the Thomistic angle, the textbooks amounted to introductory presentations of Aquinas (and Aristotle) on logic; Aquinas (and Aristotle) on the natural world; Aquinas (and Aristotle) on the living thing with emphasis on man. Some of these textbooks were good, some very good; they had a clear view of what they wanted to do and they did it remarkably well. Not all of them, God knows, but some. The general idea was that the philosophy courses represented a mounting curve; finally, the student took metaphysics. But it was questionable that the metaphysics took, or the philosophy of man, or the philosophy of nature, or logic. If it did not, if the student could not reasonably be expected to master the wide range of problems covered in all those courses, what had been accomplished? Well, he had a pretty good picture of what Aquinas had taught. He had information of how Thomistic doctrine was said to relate to carefully selected modern and contemporary views. As Aquinas said of the young who are taught metaphysics, they cannot understand it but they can repeat what they have heard. One hears the echo of Augustine. We do not send our sons to school to learn what the teacher knows. Or what Aquinas said. This curriculum was simply too ambitious; it did not, it could not, achieve its goal. An earlier chapter made it clear that I accept the notion of progression through various disciplines to a sapiential over-view as a good description of what philosophy is and of how one acquires philosophical wisdom. My present point is that I think it was a mistake to take that "order of learning" as a ready-made plan for a curriculum for undergraduates in a twentieth-century American Catholic college. I will return to my own suggestions on curricula later.

There were other conceptions of the meaning of a curriculum of undergraduate philosophy courses, but they shared with the one I mention the need for a plurality of textbooks to convey Thomistic metaphysics, psychology, ethics, etc. That is, whatever the conception of the curriculum, it responded to or called forth a set of textbooks in which a fairly well-rounded presentation of a slice of the philosophical task was given. What controlled the presentation was the author's conception of the doctrine of Aquinas. The questions were by and large the questions Aquinas asked; the answers were intended to be those Aquinas had given or would have given. The book ended with the resounding impression that that was that. Authors other than Aquinas were of course mentioned; sometimes they were treated sympathetically, usually they were not. Most often they functioned as foils for the official view being retailed. And that, really, was the trouble. The books gave the student the scoop and by the shovelful. Far too much was taken up if it were to be treated well. Why? In order to give the whole picture. One seemed always hastening on to another point. This affected the style and method, points were made inadequately, obvious difficulties hurried past. Was this the function of the instructor? His syllabus hardly allowed him to develop matters to the requisite length if philosophical assimilation, learning, were to take place.

A decade or so ago, at what was perhaps the crest of the textbook flood, there was a crescendoing criticism of textbooks. The critics did not speak with a single voice. Some said that, while philosophical instruction of the kind enshrined in textbooks was all right for seminarians, it did not meet the needs of the lay student. Others were against textbooks because they were secondary sources and what they wanted were courses taught with the text itself of Aquinas. Yet others urged a more historical basis for the philosophy curriculum, where the student would be led from ancient philosophy through medieval and into modern thinkers. Such a curriculum could use either narrative histories of philosophy or original sources. Finally, there were those who wanted neither a return to the original text of Aquinas (in English translation, to be sure) nor a curriculum in the history of philosophy. They wanted to teach phenomenology or existentialism or, more recently, analysis. That is, they wanted to replace one philosophical persuasion with another where the replacement was conceived to commend itself, apart from susbstantive grounds, because it was recent and new and timely.

The first reaction is one I have no sympathy with, and it may not have been intended to be an endorsement of seminary philosophy so much as a disarming tactic. Surely if seminary philosophy was as bad as described, it couldn't be considered to be all right for seminarians. It was not all right for anyone, least of all for future priests. Some who made this distinction did so for wider reasons; they wanted to suggest that in speaking of college courses in philosophy we needn't worry about the Church's wishes concerning Aquinas since those were directed to seminaries. My own feeling is that we should be able, even while recognizing the different purposes of seminary and college curricula in philosophy, to come up with curricula which honor the Church's wishes regarding the role of Aquinas. For I do not think that those wishes can be narrowed to directives for seminaries.

The back-to-the-texts suggestion has much more to commend it, but it does not seem to me to be an adequate answer to curricular difficulties. The historical-sequence suggestion is, I think, a counsel of despair, on a par with the remark that philosophy is what philosophers do. We still have to be given criteria for recognizing philosophers and, if an earlier argument has any force, a man's claim to be one or the historians' willingness to call him one does not settle the matter. Furthermore, although a counsel of despair, such an historical sequence seems open to the fallacy of evolutionary optimism, suggesting as it may that we have come a long distance from the Greeks, philosophically speaking. That is an assumption not every philosopher is willing to make without a dozen qualifications. Finally, to replace Thomism with existentialism or phenomenology or analysis, a suggestion which would of course be based on substantive grounds, does not really address itself to the problem before us. That problem thus far is one of style and procedure rather than one of substance; a narrow and catechetical and scholastic, in the pejorative sense, style can and has attached itself to existentialism, phenomenology, and analysis. What we want is not a rotation of vices, a shift of Isms, a new orthodoxy. What we want is a philosophical instruction which will embody the wishes of the Church on this matter. This calls for a change of style and a new look at substance, a new look at Aquinas, a timely way of being Thomistic. On a large scale, the vision of Leo XIII has not been realized; in a very real sense, therefore, Thomism has not yet been tried and, not having been tried, it cannot be said to have been found wanting.

The Leonine Revival

It is impossible, even today, to read the *Aeterni patris* of Leo XIII without the feeling that here is a challenge and invitation to Catholic thinkers of the most serious and exciting kind. Issued in 1879, this encyclical has borne some fruits, fruits so obvious that they were recognized by such non-Catholic philosophers as the American, Josiah Royce. Writing in 1903, after the death of Leo, Royce had this to say: "Many students of philosophy, of theology, and even of the natural sciences —students, I mean, who have no direct concern with any of the internal affairs of Leo's own religious body—are still forced, although outsiders, to recognize how important, for the general intellectual progress of our time, the future outcome of the whole Neo-Scholastic movement in the Catholic Church may prove. For if the process which Leo initiated continues to go unhindered, the positive results for the increase of wholesome cooperation between Catholic and non-Catholic investigators and teachers will probably be both great and helpful."[6] Royce goes on to suggest that the influence of a revived Scholastic philosophy on contemporary thinking will doubtless be mutual and that is as it should be. There are aspects of the teaching of St. Thomas he finds uneven and inadequate and he enumerates several, but by and large he expresses a sympathy and interest that one would expect from a thinker of his depth and sincerity. At the time he writes, with Leo dead, Royce expresses fears for the future of the Thomistic revival. Hoping these fears will not be realized, he concludes, "But what an admirable opportunity for a genuine spiritual growth will be lost if Leo's revival of Catholic philosophy has even its first fruits cut off, and is not permitted to bear the still richer fruit that, in case it is unhindered, it will some day surely bring forth."[7]

Royce's expectation that the Catholic philosopher has something distinctive to contribute to the general work of philosophy is one that continues to be shared by the vast majority of non-Catholic thinkers who take any interest in the matter. Surely it would be the depth of irony if this conviction were lost by the Catholic philosopher, if the Catholic philosopher regarded his involvement in the intellectual life as indistinguishable from that of non-Catholic Chris-

tian or Jewish philosophers and even from that of agnostic
and atheist philosophers. Any such effort on the part of the
Catholic philosopher to appear indistinguishable is met with
wary amusement by his colleagues who remember, even
when the Catholic forgets, that in the person of the Catholic philosopher there must be a meeting of faith and knowledge. The effort to take on the dominant coloration of contemporary philosophizing, with a concomitant and strident
critique of the substance of traditional Catholic philosophy,
if it is motivated by zeal, as it often is, seems to me destined to
have the opposite of its desired effect. We will have come to
an odd pass if the believer has to be reminded by the non-
believer that faith is a pervasive and undeniable guide to the
philosophizing of the believer. Far from being impressed by
attempts at such an impossible abstraction of philosophizing
from faith, the non-believer will tend to suspect that the
faith of his Catholic colleague is empty or disappearing and,
when one considers the anguished condition of many who
have attempted the abstraction, it is hard not to see precisely
this danger lurking over the horizon. The minimal response
to the Church's suggestions concerning the Catholic's en-
gagement in philosophy requires a prolonged reflection on
just this matter. *Philosophandum in fide* can hardly be construed as the option of some excessively docile Catholics; if it
is stated as an exhortation, this is only because it is a reminder
to do consciously and well what one, as a Catholic, cannot
fail to do. Whatever others may think, the Catholic who
regards his faith as an impediment to philosophy, as restric-
tive and confining, is on the way to having his philosophy
become an impediment to his faith. *Videte ne quis vos decip-
iat per philosophiam:* watch out lest anyone lead you astray
through philosophy, St. Paul warned.[8] How tragic if that
someone should be oneself. Revealed truth is a tremendously

liberating and fortifying factor in the philosophizing of the Christian. The Catholic philosopher who does not reflect on his condition, who does not grasp and welcome that truth, is open to the kind of fideism against which Paul VI warns. But with fideism faith becomes unreasonable and it is at least dubious that one whose vocation is the life of reason will long adhere to something he mistakenly consigns to the region of the absurd and irrational.

These are things I feel constrained to say, without authority, God knows, but with, I hope, the best of motives. If Catholic philosophy has not been all it should be, it is up to Catholics to remedy the situation. This is what the Church expects of us; it is, I think, what we expect of ourselves. My present suggestion, relevant to any effort at dialogue with non-Catholics, is that this is precisely what our non-Catholic colleagues expect of us. To refuse the challenge is a disservice not only to ourselves and to the Church but also to our non-Catholic colleagues who are right to expect better of us. This was certainly the invitation issued to Catholics by Leo XIII in *Aeterni patris*. Was it accepted?

Consider the following assessment of Father James Weisheipl. "It is a social historical fact that the hope of Leo XIII has never been universally realized in Catholic colleges, universities and seminaries. Not even the ardent efforts of St. Pius X, Benedict XV, Pius XI, or Pius XII were able to effect anything more than a closed, safe, and sterile Thomism, imposed by legislative authority. Legislation did not stimulate a return to the true thought and spirit of St. Thomas relevant to our day. Legislation led rather to the production of safe textbooks that demolished adversaries (*sententiae oppositae*) with presumptuous conviction. But this merely led students to pass easily, as Pius XII noted in 1950, 'from despising scholastic theology to the neglect of and even con-

tempt for the teaching authority of the Church itself, which
gives such authoritative approval to scholastic theology.' Pius
XII might just as easily have used the terms 'philosophy' or
'Thomism' in this context. Until the program of Leo XIII
is seriously attempted in a thorough and spontaneous manner, there will always be zealous priests and laymen who
react to what they only half understand. Reactions against
Thomism in the past half-century have been, in fact, to a
pseudo-Thomism, a half-understood St. Thomas."[9]

Father Weisheipl takes a very dim view of Church legislation on the matter of Thomism, although he is careful to
point out the factual situations that called it forth. He laments
the atmosphere that was created by that legislation and the
political machinations to which it gave rise. He goes so far
as to draw an analogy between the Third Reich and "the
reign of terror" that existed from 1910 onwards. He senses
the dawn of a new era with John XXIII and Vatican II, but
a new era, be it noted, for Thomism, a Thomism in the
spirit of *Aeterni patris* and of Thomas Aquinas himself.

Those who were subjected to some version of the rigid,
catechetical Thomism described above may be impatient
with attempts to dissociate Thomas from that Thomism. This
effort may seem a belated face-saving one undertaken by
those who have a vested interest in retaining power behind
a hastily revised image. Was that so-called sterile Thomism
all that untrue to St. Thomas Aquinas? Since this reaction is
both predictable and understandable, something will be
gained by pointing to a number of ways in which the Thomism to be rejected was really untrue to Thomas. Since the
objections have to do, for the most part, with style and
method and scope, it is principally to these that I will address
myself.

Aquinas and Jargon.—The question of philosophical terminology is complex and difficult. Peirce has a passage in his papers entitled "The Ethics of Terminology"; in it he recommends that philosophers proceed as do botanists and devise labels from Greek and Latin for their key positions and tenets. Peirce is characteristically straightforward in this suggestion which would lead, I think, to the apotheosis of philosophical jargon. Nevertheless, he is addressing himself to a commonly recognized fact about philosophical literature. That literature is in large part written with the vocabulary of ordinary life, but the philosopher employs terms from the ordinary language in an extraordinary way, so extraordinary in fact that one who took the terms as they are usually understood would miss the whole point of what the philosopher is trying to say. To overcome the ambiguities within the natural language and the further ambiguity created by using its vocabulary for technical purposes, Peirce suggests in effect that philosophers create a unique terminology from which ambiguity can be systematically excluded. Similar suggestions with a more limited purpose are usually made in introductions to logic textbooks. The advantage of a formal language in doing logic, the argument runs, is that we are immediately free of the ambiguities of natural speech.

The logician's claim has more plausibility than Peirce's more sweeping recipe, but in many respects the formal language of logic merely postpones a difficulty. When we are concerned, not simply with logical reasoning, but with reasoning logically, the problem of the interpretation of the symbols presents itself. Outside of logic, our concern is not with logical sysmbols, but with substantive matters and those substantive matters may very well be the things ordinary men know well enough to name and talk about. A translation is in order, therefore, and one that presents a dual difficulty. For there is the prior task of translating from the natural into the

formal language and the subsequent one of translating from
the formal back into the natural language. Whichever end of
the process we look at, it becomes quite clear that the formal
language of logic cannot be commended as just of itself
overcoming ambiguities within the natural language. That
ambiguity has to be overcome before symbols can be invoked and the overcoming therefore is a task within natural
language and carried on in terms of natural language. Peirce's
suggestion loses its attractiveness so soon as we attend to the
difficulties that would be involved in learning the technical
language he proposes. In order to learn it, the elements of
the technical language have to be put into relation with the
natural language each of us has been speaking since childhood and this entails, or so it seems to me, that a technical
term must always be able to be cashed in the currency of the
natural language, some phrase at least of the natural language serving as descriptive of what it means. One could
imagine a technical language where the exchange could go on
for a time in terms of scrip, but sooner or later the whole
system has to be related to the Fort Knox of ordinary language. If not, how could it be learned? Well, counter-sug-
gestions are possible, I know, but I will ease the matter to a
tentative close here because I am convinced the point I am
making could continue to be made in the face of such further
considerations as occur to me.

What is the straightforward alternative to Peirce's suggestion? It is the conscious and reflected-upon alternative of
Aristotle and Aquinas as well as many others, the unconscious alternative of most philosophers. If philosophy is the
continuation of a kind of thinking few men could fail to engage in, if it is an attempt to do well the inquiring which is
definitive of man, this formal and reflexive effort must
always be regarded as continuous with that spontaneous ef-

fort. The spontaneous effort is expressed in the natural languages men devise in society; the formal effort can be carried on in that same language. When a philosopher makes use of the natural language, he will want to select terms from it which express an awareness or knowledge connected with the knowledge he has acquired. Unless he does this, unless he is able to put the meaning he attaches to, say, "form" and "act" and "substance" into relation with the meaning those terms already have and show why he selected the terms he did rather than others, his language will not be an instrument of communication. The function of the language philosophers use, in short, is to enable men to move from what they already know to what they don't yet know and if there is a dependence of the latter on the former, this dependence can be enshrined by retaining the same vocabulary. It is not often noticed how severely limited the philosophical vocabulary of Aquinas is; how very few terms it contains which don't already have a meaning and use in ordinary Latin.

The philosophical terminology arrived at in the way I have sketched is a deliberate courting of ambiguity. Since it is deliberate, or systematic, it must be constantly alluded to in order that it not become an impediment. Book Delta of the *Metaphysics* of Aristotle is subtitled, in the Oxford translation, a Philosophical Lexicon, and another English edition of that work actually places Book Delta, or Five, at the beginning. In either case, the suggestion seems to be that the book contains Aristotle's technical language, the jargon of his philosophy. But it is quite clear to the reader of that book that the devising of the terminology is one of the most important philosophical tasks Aristotle ever undertook, that its importance lies precisely in his concern *not* to employ a jargon or technical language in the remote sense implied by those two English editions. For, as is obvious, Aristotle's conception of philosophical vocabulary rests upon any number of substantive philosophical positions: the nature of language, the question of meaning, the order of learning, etc. Aristotle's view of philosophical terminology cannot be separated from his vision of what man is, the trajectory of human knowledge, the function or functions of language. We spoke earlier of the opening considerations of Aristotle's *Metaphysics* and pointed out that he there calls our attention to the primacy, in our lives, of the practical, of the technical in the root sense. Given that obvious point about what it means to be a man, unavoidable consequences follow for philosophical language. If there is an area, a dimension of human existence, that no man can fail to understand and if his performance there involves and is enshrined in language, any effort to lead men from what they already know to what they do not yet know must pay careful and sustained attention to that common stratum of awareness.

Was Aristotle so naïve as to think that this common knowledge of men was clearly contained in natural language? Surely not, since he spends much time, in his analysis of natural language, of ordinary language, removing impediments to seeing its fundamental, ineradicable content. If the Greek language, as actually spoken, both contained and covered up what every man knows, modern languages are vehicles of far more freight and do not easily lend themselves to employment beyond ordinary ones. It is often pointed out that sophisticated uses of language, philosophical and/or scientific interpretation of terms, filter back into common usage; ordinary language can thus seem to be the repository of fossilized concepts, familiar but hardly evident notions. Think of Korzybski and the Anti-Aristotelian Society. It is the thesis of this semantic school that ordinary language is vitiated by the influence on it of Aristotelian conceptions. Aristotle's point was just the opposite, that his conceptions and uses of language were controlled by what men knew before his arrival on the scene and independently of anything he might say. In Korzybski's favor, we can recall the twofold aspect of "common sense" discussed earlier.

This is not the place to engage in any sustained discussion of the nature of language. I had to say as much as I have in order to provide the necessary background for understanding Aquinas' conception of a desirable philosophical vocabulary. On these matters, his views are one with those of Aristotle, whose psychology and doctrine on language he accepts. What this means for philosophical instruction is that it must always be kept in a close and warm relationship with ordinary language. Really to teach philosophy, really to teach anything, is to begin where the student is, with the certitudes he has prior to instruction and with the language he ordinarily employs to express that antecedent knowledge. Now, aren't some of the objections to the previously regnant Thomism really objections to the unreal language in which it was embodied? Whether one was embarrassed by it or took a fleeting and perverse pride in it, the student knew his parents could not have the slightest inkling of what he was saying if he should quote to them a passage from his philosophy text, even—perhaps particularly—if it were in English. The recognition that one shared their ignorance was not exactly an exhilarating experience. What did it all *mean?* What relevance did it have for the common concerns and language of men? These were not silly, inapposite questions. They amounted to an essential and devastating criticism—and one Aquinas himself would have made of this Thomism.

Let us not suppose that the Church favored this sort of jargon. In *Humani generis*, Pius XII had this to say: "However, even in these fundamental questions, we may clothe our

philosophy in a more convenient dress, make it more vigor-
ous with a more effective terminology, divest it of certain
scholastic aids found less useful, prudently enrich it with the
fruits of progress of the human mind."[10] One could multiply
such suggestions about philosophical terminology. Does this
mean that *being, cause, substance, form, matter*, and so forth,
are to be expunged from our philosophical vocabulary? Surely
not. They continue to function in our language when we
are not doing philosophy. But they have taken on any number of what C. S. Lewis called, in a different but related area,
dangerous senses.[11] There is a vast task of analysis and sifting
of ordinary usage required, a task that may be performed
piecemeal or in a sustained though still limited way, if those
dangerous senses are to be avoided and the desired sense recognized. It is scarcely a matter of chance that many philosophers today feel impelled to peel away the layers of ordinary
usage in order to get at ineradicable senses and uses of common terms. This task is undertaken by thinkers as different
as Heidegger and Wittgenstein and if their immediate pro-
cedures differ, if their ultimate objectives differ yet more,
anyone can come to appreciate the importance and necessity
of what they are up to. The chaos created by conflicting
philosophical traditions has come to be mirrored in ordinary
language and we are in danger of being cheated out of our
primary certitudes. Analysis and phenomenology, in different ways, provide invaluable aids to removing impediments
to seeing what we all already know. In many different ways,
contemporary philosophers can be regarded as re-examining
the starting point, regaining the starting point, from which
philosophy traditionally set out. The difficulties within Thomism, within Catholic philosophy generally, are not confined
to it; they are part of a widespread malaise where even the
evident is felt to be obscure. The Catholic can recognize the

difficulties, he has had his share in creating them, but he is spared the vertigo of thinking that after the layers of the fantastic and familiar have been peeled away, we will be left, as with a Lockian onion, with discarded skin and no substance.

Chatter and Informing.—Buried away in Aquinas' discussion of the angels—who nowadays reads the Angelic Doctor on angels?—is a distinction pertinent to what we have been saying. He asks if angels can talk to one another. (At this point, I imagine a certain kind of reader lurches or shudders. My God, how baroque! Perhaps. But what prompts the question is the *Epistle to the Corinthians*, I, 13:1: "If I should speak with the tongue of men and angels. . . .") Aquinas establishes the nature of the metaphor involved here[12] and then, relying on the notion of a hierarchy of angels, asks if a lower angel can speak to a higher one. I am not presently interested in the context but in the distinction Aquinas draws between talk that is mere talk (*locutio*) and talk that is informative (*illuminatio*). Truly informative talk is independent of the informer, since what he says is referred to principles, knowledge of which the learner may be supposed to have. "But the manifestation of those things which depend on the will of the one who knows them cannot be called informative but merely talk. For example, if someone tells another, I want to learn that, I want to do this or that. . . . To know what you might wish does not serve to perfect my mind nor does to know what you know, but only the way things are."[13] The connection of this with earlier discussions will, I trust, be seen. We do not send our children to school to learn what the teacher knows. We do not study philosophy to learn what a thinker holds, what Aquinas said. No doubt there is a fine line to be drawn between the virtue of gratitude and the vice of quoting; it is the rare philosopher who will not give citations, references to his reading, particularly when his reading has helped him to gain a position. If one did not acknowledge such debts, we would feel him deficient. There is a basis for the copyright laws. Yet, finally, of course, the point of philosophy is not who said it, but what is said and the reasons for saying it. Once more this is a tricky area. The ideal may seem austere, altogether too austere. Is the reading of history and biography to be proscribed? Is our interest in the story of our children's day somehow suspect since all we get is a *narratio singularium*, the events of which detain us because this is Junior speaking? No consequences so loathsome as these follow on the distinction made. My point in invoking it is that it makes it as clear as could be desired that Aquinas provides no warrant for our being interested in what he said as what he said. And is that last sentence *locutio* or *illuminatio?*

Problems and Theses.—The trouble with reducing what Thomas taught to a number of theses is that conclusions can seem to be enshrined at the expense of the arguments that support them. But of course a conclusion is only as good as its supporting argument. There is no inherent fault in a pedagogical method which would proceed by saying this is the way it is and now here are the reasons for the claim. But what can be absent from such a procedure, and not merely temporarily, is the question that at least originally must have controlled it. What possible interest could we have in an answer, even if accompanied by supporting reasons, if it had never occurred to us to ask the question? Surely the main part of philosophical instruction is to encourage inquiry, to guide it, to make sure good questions are being asked. The term used to signify this today (ungrammatically, as it happens, since an adjective is employed as a substantive) is the problematic. We must, we are urged, first work up the problematic. Grammar aside, it is a salutary reminder. And isn't this, again, part of the criticism of the Thomism that has prevailed? Is this what the Church is recommending when, among other things, she urges us to pay particular attention to the method of St. Thomas? Well, what was the method of St. Thomas? That it was a method of inquiry is stylistically clear from the *Summa theologiae*. The titles of the articles are precisely questions; the major divisions of the work are *quaestiones*. A question, for Aquinas, was the expression of indecision before possible answers, so the question embodies inquiry, wonder, searching. Furthermore, the question is answered, the problem resolved, by putting into play as live possibilities a number of alternative positions. Even those who read the *Summa theologiae* seem sometimes to miss the dialectical, problematic procedure of that work. It was to counteract this, we may suppose, that Professor Otto Bird wrote an article on how to read an article in the *Summa*.[14] Teaching should be problematic, inquiring, dialectical, something carried on in terms of the interplay of possible answers, all of which can usually be shown to cast some light on the matter at hand. The procedure of Aquinas has not characterized the Thomism many would reject. One must admit that theirs is a fundamentally Thomistic criticism.

A final word about scope. While there are obvious limitations on the sources that can be usefully brought into play in discussing a given philosophical question, there seems to have been an unnecessary narrowing of interest on the part of Thomists. Furthermore, even when the range of sources was broadened, the impression was seldom given that the authors referred to could have any substantial contribution to make. All too often they were brought in merely to be chastised. Now maybe they needed chastisement; maybe much of what they wrote was both absurd and dangerous. But consider again the manner of Aquinas.[15] One reads him with the growing awareness that he was in principle interested in anything available to him, from whatever source it came; moreover, the sympathy with which he reads authors whose fundamental tenets are opposed to his own, the value he insists on finding wherever he reads, is something almost unique in the history of philosophy. Try if you will to imagine an Aquinas alive today who would not be well versed in Wittgenstein, Ryle, Wisdom, Russell, Whitehead, Heidegger, Jaspers, Sartre, and so forth. That is almost as impossible as imagining Aquinas a Thomist in the sense that designation has sometimes had. We are still proceeding here on a fairly superficial level, but the spirit which guided Aquinas' own intellectual labor is the polar opposite of that which would, considerations of time and talent aside, limit the range of authors to be read or approach with a prejudiced mind any author, even when his terminology and approach are unfamiliar and difficult. I have always been struck by Aquinas' commentary on the *Liber de causis*, the Neoplatonic work that derived from Proclus—a discovery owed to a piece of detective work by Aquinas himself. The starting point of that work, its vocabulary and style, are such that one might be prepared for an unsympathetic reading of it by Aquinas. But just the opposite happens. Moreover, his commentary contains a large number of references to Aristotle, attesting to a supreme effort to read this work in the light of positions Aquinas considered to be already established. The upshot of the commentary is that Thomas sees the Neoplatonic emanation metaphysics as the possibility opened up by the Aristotelian ascent from below. Thus two initially conflicting metaphysical views are shown to be complementary to one another.

A consequence of some of the features of the sterile Thomism we have been examining is that at times readers of Aquinas lost the sense of the varying force of arguments and put on a par with firmly established positions others which are at best likely or probable. I suppose it was this sort of thing that led critics of Thomism to ask Thomists if they thought everything Aquinas had written is true. To say, "No, he quoted a lot," was seldom, I found, received for the feeble humor it tried to be. But the accusation veiled in the question was so absurd and sweeping that one would have liked to believe a quip could do service as a reply. Any philosophical benefit derived from reading Aquinas, to repeat a point, consists in freeing oneself from the fact that Aquinas said it. Like others who have profited from their study of an author, Thomists may sometimes have seemed excessively reluctant to discard an argument of Aquinas merely because it was dense and difficult. But none of this need have been tantamount to treating the *opera omnia* of Aquinas as a repository of the truth and nothing but the truth, with its ultimate warrant the fact that Aquinas was the author.

Perhaps these few remarks will suffice as a justification of the claim that many of the things which have been objected to in traditional so-called Thomism could be objected to on Thomistic grounds. It is not meaningless to say, therefore, that a rejection of such Thomism has little or nothing to do with the teaching of Thomas Aquinas.

A Substantive Response

We suggested a minimal response to the Church's recommendation of St. Thomas which turned being a Thomist into being a man who makes an effort to conjoin reason and faith, and that would seem to be the unavoidable task of a Catholic engaged in intellectual matters. Because many would be content with this minimal response because of a bad experience with what was called Thomism, we went on to accept descriptions of the Thomism criticized and agreed that it ought to be rejected. However, to reject such a Thomism is not, as we tried to show, a rejection of Aquinas. That last point was made in terms of style, approach, and manner of philosophizing because the objections to Thomism and its consequent rejection are often made in terms of such factors. The open manner of philosophizing we attributed to Aquinas, while it is his authentic manner and must be an essential component of any future Thomism, cannot be thought to characterize Thomism in any substantial sense. It is a necessary but not a sufficient condition for a substantial Thomism. Surely a concern with philosophical terminology, paying attention to the exigencies of pedagogy, an irenic and sympathetic attitude to whatever philosophical document are not attitudes confined to Aquinas. Thus even if this open spirit be added to the kind of minimal response suggested earlier, we are still far from any notion of what Thomism is in a substantive sense.

We have reached, therefore, a difficult point in our essay and one the adequate treatment of which would require far more space than we intend to use here and a far different manner of procedure. There is little point in listing a series of key positions of Aquinas that would make up a substantive Thomism, though such a list could be made. Included in that list would be such items as his establishment of the spirituality of the human soul and of its immortality, together with such allied positions as the difference between intellection and sensation and the manner in which intellection is dependent upon sensation. All of this would lead to a statement of the essential realism of Aquinas. Now even to mention the philo-

sophical questions associated with realism should be sufficient indication of the difficulty I am facing here. The term
"realism" has become so ambiguous that it makes next to
little sense to say of Thomas that he held for realism. Royce,
in the essay mentioned, cited the changing scholastic attitude
toward Kant and seemed to be calling attention to the
amount of "idealism" that could be assimilated by "realism."
A list such as is envisaged would have to include Aquinas'
proofs of the existence of God, his teaching on the basic
principles of morality and the nature of the moral decision.
Once more, phrases like "natural law" and "practical syllo-
gism" do not wear their meanings on their faces; they mean
wildly different things to different people. What I am saying
is that any list that could be drawn up would have to be accompanied by a rather thorough commentary if its meaning
were to be clear. Even if such difficulties could be overcome,
I doubt that very widespread agreement could be reached as
to what would constitute a list of the essential teachings of
Aquinas. This does not really bother me. The day of such
lists is, I should hope, behind us. The day of testing the ade-
quacy of the Thomism of others, their Thomisticity, as it
were, is behind us. To engage in that sort of thing is to be
drawn away from the philosophical task, to lose the spirit of
philosophizing, to want to identify the "true believers" in an
area where belief is not the point. Anyone can consult the ecclesiastical documents to find short lists of the Thomistic positions which have prompted the Church to single out St.
Thomas in the way she has. What I want to say is this. To
be really meaningful, the term "Thomism" must include
more than what is involved in the minimal response and openness in philosophizing mentioned above. I have certain ideas
as to what a minimal but substantive Thomism would
amount to, but I am unwilling to lay it out lest it be con-

strued as some kind of standard for others. The matter cannot be left here, of course, but to carry it beyond this point must be a group rather than an individual decision.

Let me try to clarify the preceding, rather obscure paragraph. Throughout this chapter I have been failing to distinguish between two types of response to the Church's wishes that we undertake the study of philosophy under the guidance of Aquinas, types that could be called the personal response and the institutional response. It was to my advantage not to make this distinction earlier; it would be to my disadvantage not to make it now. The Church documents in question are, by and large, addressed to bishops primarily or to the heads of religious institutions, universities, and so forth, but beyond these stated addressees they speak to the faithful at large. Each of us must, therefore, ask, What is their meaning for me? Part of what I have been trying to say is that I should find it difficult to understand why any Catholic would simply ignore what the Church has to say here. And, although I accept as a possibility the interpretation of Aquinas as a symbol of an effort the Christian intellectual must inevitably make, while I suggest that there is a description of the spirit of Thomism which is relatively independent of the substance of what Aquinas taught, it is nevertheless my opinion that every Catholic philosopher has a special obligation to give Aquinas himself a sympathetic reading. I say a special obligation because it is generally incumbent upon philosophers to read the writings of acknowledged giants in the field and it goes without saying that such a reading should be sympathetic. When a philosopher is a Catholic, when his church has repeatedly and in unmistakable terms directed his attention to the writings of Aquinas, it is surely not extreme to suggest that he should heed this advice and give a privileged status to the views of Aquinas on philosophical problems he

takes up, where Aquinas has views. I have often marveled at
the docility of converts like Jacques Maritain and Edith Stein,
who, though already formed philosophers, turned themselves
to a prolonged study of St. Thomas Aquinas. Here as elsewhere the behavior of converts is instructive for the cradle
Catholic, for one insufficiently grateful for familiar blessings.

When things are transposed to this level, when a Catholic
philosopher reads Aquinas seriously and sympathetically, the
only controlling criteria are those of reason. None of the
Thomistic positions I mentioned above when I wasn't draw-
ing up a list is uncontroverted; the only meaningful way any
Thomistic position or argument can be philosophically assimilated is by an interplay of positions, by taking particular
account of criticisms of Aquinas. The proofs of the existence
of God are an obvious instance. These proofs have been subjected to severe criticism and some of these criticisms are important and timely. The serious student of Aquinas has to
take them into account. What will the upshot of this be? Does
one who is beginning the study of these proofs have to be
assured that those proofs can withstand any conceivable criticism? I may think they can, and let us hope that if I think
so my conviction is based on a sustained and serious look at
actual criticisms of them. What I am trying to say is that
we must not define a serious study of such proofs in terms
of a conviction that can only be the result of a serious study.
A Catholic may become convinced, after studying these
proofs, that they are invalid. If he publishes his criticisms,
another may wish to dispute with him. My point is that we
cannot and should not even faintly suggest that the first man
is somehow remiss in his obligations as a Catholic. What we
have to keep absolutely clear is that there is no such thing as
official orthodoxy so far as substantive philosophical arguments and positions go, unless of course a philosophical po-

sition is in open and flagrant opposition to revealed truth. The Thomistic proofs for the existence of God—need it be said?—are not part of revealed truth.

All the Church asks, all we need ask of ourselves, is that we give St. Thomas a careful and sympathetic reading. The only grounds for accepting any element of his philosophy will be evidence and argument. It seems obvious to me that underlying the Church's recommendation of Aquinas is her acceptance of a long tradition of esteem in which Aquinas has been held, the assumption that his arguments will, a large part of them, hold. And, of course, her proper judgment that what he taught is in remarkable conformity with the faith. Once more, there is no suggestion here that we must believe Aquinas in the strong sense of believe, that we must believe in the strong sense that such and such a proof of his is valid. The validity of a philosophical proof is a matter of judgment, not of faith.

I think it unlikely that anyone can study St. Thomas without philosophical profit. Some students will find more and others less that is acceptable in Aquinas. My point about personal response and my unwillingness to draw up a list of Thomistic positions has to do with just this possibility. One may be in accord with St. Thomas on some points and in disagreement with him on others. Far better really to hold a few philosophical positions, which happen also to have been held by Aquinas, which happen to have been arrived at by a study of Aquinas, than to adhere to a whole host of un-examined philosophical tenets which one cannot adequately communicate or defend. Of two men, one of whom holds to X number of Thomistic theses as if they constituted a *credo*, theses he cannot sustain against relevant objections, while the other holds one or two positions in common with Aquinas but holds them philosophically, rationally—well, it would not be difficult to say which is the better philosopher, which is the better Thomist.

If I were to try to sum up what I have been trying to say about the personal response to the Church's wishes concerning Aquinas, this is what I would say. It seems to me that every Catholic philosopher has an antecedent obligation of a special kind to study Aquinas seriously and with sympathy. From that point on, he is under no obligation as to what the outcome of that study will be. He is under no obligation to agree with Aquinas. To suggest otherwise is to deny the very nature of philosophy. It is because many have sensed that suggestion in the attitude of Thomists that they have turned away from what is indeed their obligation, namely to take St. Thomas seriously into account in their philosophizing. For what comfort they may derive from it, I am suggesting that this does not entail that they take Thomists seriously.

When we realize that what the Church has had to say about the teaching of St. Thomas calls for an antecedent deference to him of a special kind but is not a prediction that there will be a consequent deference, based on philosophical assimilation, or, if there is, that this will be homogeneous and on all points the same, we realize what I should like to think no one ever seriously doubted, that Thomism must meet the same demands in the intellectual market place as any other philosophical position. This does not mean that the non-Catholic may have to be convinced of its value while the Catholic accepts it on trust. There is only one way to be a Thomist and that is by being a philosopher and there is but one set of demands that must be met by the philosopher, whether or not he is a Catholic. If Thomists have in the past seemed to demand of their fellow Catholics adherence to philosophical tenets on other than philosophical grounds, then Thomists have been grievously wrong. If men have thought they were philosophers who could not sustain the views they held, then they have been mistaken and it is criminal if they covered up their deficiencies with the label of Thomism. It is laudable to be alert to the advice of the Church on how we should begin the study of philosophy; it is culpable to equate the antecedent attitude with the finished product.

I hope that my Catholic reader will agree with what I have said earlier about our advantages as philosophers, advantages which derive from faith and from the fact that the advice we receive about the study of philosophy comes from a source as trustworthy as the ordinary magisterium of the Church. It is equally clear that these advantages would become disadvantages if we thought they exempted us from the difficult task philosophizing is. I suspect it is because, for some, Thomism seemed the enshrinement of the view that, within philosophy, the Catholic is not subject to the same demands as any philosopher, that Thomism has become a symbol of what must be cast aside. The study of St. Thomas should never have become a synonym for intellectual lethargy and sham. Surely it is the task of those who have learned from that study to redeem Thomism from this misunderstanding.

On the level of the personal response to Aquinas, it is impossible to predict what the Thomism of the future will be. However, it should be safe to predict that what we will move toward is not Thomism but Thomisms, any number of ways of truly and philosophically profiting from the study of Aquinas. This plurality of Thomisms will not simply be a function of diversity of talent; it will also be the result of the unavoidable division of philosophical labor. The interests of some will lead them into the philosophy of science; of others into ethics, into social and political philosophy; yet others will be principally concerned with philosophical anthropology. Some will devote themselves chiefly to theory of knowledge and metaphysics; others to logic, semantics, and allied topics. What these multiple efforts will have in common, insofar as they can be called Thomisms, is that the philosophers who undertake them will know Aquinas well and, knowing him well, will have taken on his spirit which entails that they are in principle open and interested and sympathetic to whatever has been written on their principal interest. Furthermore, having taken on the spirit of Aquinas, they will retain the view that the ultimate import of any special knowledge is the aid it can give us in coming to know God. It goes without saying that many questions which occupy Catholic philosophers were undreamt of by Aquinas or were posed by him in a different or more limited fashion. Thomistic positions will doubtless be altered by being put into relation with other views, later views, different vantage points. But of course the task of the philosopher who has learned some things from his study of Aquinas is not to show that he can learn nothing from anyone else, it is not to defend at all costs, whatever further considerations are brought to bear, what Aquinas said. I suspect that Catholic philosophers of the future, all of whom may be called Thomists in some meaningful sense of the term, will bear only a family resemblance to one another rather than the cooky-cutter identity that seems to have been the expectation of some past devotees of Aquinas. As we move away from the baleful influence of the suggestion that there is a substantively orthodox Catholic philosophy, as our philosophizing becomes livelier and, while in continuity with what Aquinas learned, yet distant from what he achieved, we will be on our way toward the Thomism envisaged by *Aeterni patris*. We will not scrutinize one another for departures from orthodoxy, but attend to the arguments. We may as Catholics know how we should begin the study of philosophy, we may have thanks to our faith a tremendous aid and impetus to philosophizing, but who of us can predict what the outcome or outcomes will be?

Institutional Responses

If on the level of personal response to the Church's advice, there are good and sufficient reasons for refraining from listing an array of philosophical tenets which anyone must accept if he is to be regarded as taking Aquinas seriously as a philosopher, the matter is rather more difficult when we turn to institutional responses. Is there a curriculum for Departments of Philosophy in Catholic colleges laid out somewhere in the heavens of orthodoxy? Curricula are or should be the embodiment of collective decisions by philosophers as to how the young may best be instructed in philosophy. If that is so, institutional responses to the desires of the Church will reflect the personal response to those desires made by the philosophers who are the faculty of a department. Those who have survived some years of departmental meetings devoted to the philosophy curriculum, those who have been put to the ultimate test of serving on committees formed for the purpose of revising a curriculum, will appreciate that any easy answers to the problems they have faced are hardly worth the laughter they would provoke. It goes without saying that discussions of philosophy curricula in Catholic colleges must, and without apology, take into account the extra-philosophical demands of faith. The Catholic philosopher who views his philosophizing in conjunction with his own faith has an obligation to introduce his students to philosophy in such a way that they too see the Christian context of philosophizing. Included in that context, for those who must worry about curriculum, is the matter of the Church's recommendation of St. Thomas as a sure guide of our philosophizing, particularly at the outset. That recognition does not bring with it a ready-made, four-course curriculum; it does not entail a particular sequence of courses; it does not demand the use of a certain kind of textbook or of English translations of Aquinas. It does not even require, finally, the mention of Aquinas' name in a course in philosophy.

The last remark is a concession to a far-out and mythical demand, of course. However, although I think it would be contrived, I can imagine a course given by one who has learned things from Aquinas who yet argued for those positions with his students while using only documents by other thinkers who made the same points. My own view of the substantive value of Aquinas' teaching is that few of his tenets are peculiar to him; indeed, I would find it exceedingly odd if that were the case. In ethics, for example, it is perfectly possible to treat a fair number of themes and employ a wide variety of readings, none of them in Aquinas, and argue for positions substantively identical with those Aquinas held. I see no reason to proceed in this way, of course, but neither do I see any impediment to doing so. My point is that, on the level of what I am calling the institutional response, there is practically nothing we *have* to do in our philosophy offerings, whether in the matter of number of courses, sequence of courses, content and methods of courses, in order to be said to be taking seriously into account the wishes of the Church. Just as there is no orthodox philosophy, so there is no orthodox curriculum.

This is not an invitation to an unserious approach to the curriculum of our philosophy departments. On the contrary, it is to direct our attention to where the seriousness lies. These matters cannot be settled by appeal to official documents. They must be settled by discussion and argument, by compromise and consensus. Welcome, in short, to the real world. The guidelines for these decisions, from the point of view of the denominational character of our colleges, are broad and permissive. Here too we have to get rid of the suggestion that there is an official answer to the vexed and difficult problems we face. We should be able to assume that no suggestions which come from a member of a philosophy department in a Catholic college will amount to jeopardizing the religious values to be safeguarded. When that assumption is made, and it is a safe one, it is more clearly recognized that views must be sustained by arguments and communicable reasons. We may be convinced that a colleague is making crazy suggestions without feeling a compulsion to tune up the wrack. What we must seek is not the safe and closed and sterile, but the open and intellectually lively. The best kind of philosophy for a Catholic college is the best kind of philosophy. It is that simple and that complex. Perhaps these few remarks will suffice to excuse me from offering a master plan for the philosophy curriculum in the Catholic college. I could not, and do not wish to, make my personal views prevail in my own university. This does not cause me to worry about the future of Western civilization, though other things do. In sum, no one can predict or prescribe what institutional responses to the wishes of the Church will be. My guess is that, like life itself, they will be various.

If the institutional response to the Church's wishes, which is embodied in the curriculum of the philosophy department, is the product of collective decision and thus ultimately reflects the personal responses to those wishes by the individual members of the department, the hiring policy of our

Catholic colleges must be both enlightened and prudent. Prospective members must of course accept the nature of the Catholic college and the legitimate if peculiar demands it makes upon its faculty. If this acceptance were merely the acceptance of external limitations and answered to no personal and free acceptance, matters could become impossibly complicated in many segments of the college, perhaps particularly in areas like philosophy. Catholics may dispute among themselves about the nature and degree of faith's influence on the practical task of teaching, but if the dispute within a Catholic college came to turn on the very legitimacy of the influence it would be unsettleable. For such a dispute could only be settled by conversion and that is the necessary consequence of no argument. An atheist, for example, would find life uncomfortable in the philosophy department of a Catholic college and it would be naïve to regard his discomfort as the result of an infringement of academic freedom. As sometimes defined, "academic freedom" would lead only to chaos. That is why, I suppose, its more hot-eyed advocates can find it not at all or only imperfectly existent in academe as we know it. More pertinent to our present point is the fact that the member of a philosophy department must have a say in such matters as the curriculum. But discussions of curricula are in large part practical and entail decisions which appeal not only to the principles of a given discipline but also to far wider matters. The wider matter at issue in Catholic colleges is a belief in God, a recognition of the teaching authority of the Church, a vision of reality. One who cannot accept the appeals that must often be made to that wider context will thereby feel restricted by truths he does not accept. This is something which must be taken into account on both sides when additions to the faculty are contemplated. And, if previous points have been made at all, such a reminder is in no way either a plea or warrant for unphilosophical philosophy.

But it is not the restrictions of our situation that should be dwelled on. In any institution, the hiring policy attempts to place academic pursuits in a broad context. In philosophy departments in Catholic colleges, where it is recognized that any and all philosophical contributions must be taken sympathetically into account, but where, as in any department, the practical limitations on effective response to every philosophical style and program and content are recognized, the broadest possible coverage should be striven for. This does not mean, I should think, that a departmental faculty should be seen on an analogy with a zoo, its desideratum one of each if not a pair. A department need not contain one analyst, one existentialist, one phenomenologist, one idealist, and so forth. But it should contain some men whose principal interest is analysis, others whose principal interest is phenomenology, and so forth. If a philosophical style or content required a committed adherent to get a fair hearing, things will have degenerated miserably. Thomism, as I have been trying to commend it in these past few pages, seems to me the best hope of getting beyond the level of factions and schools and systems of philosophy. The Thomism I envisage is not one school among others. It is the attempt to move out from a proved base in many directions, to assimilate, to grow, to renew itself as well as to correct misadventures, to be always open at the operative end of thinking. Nor is this a private vision, if I read *Aeterni patris* correctly, if I have caught the sense of the many ecclesiastical documents having to do with the role of Thomas Aquinas. We are not being invited to elect for a system among systems, because Thomism, while principled and systematic, is simply not a system. It has substantive content, but that very substantive content makes it more visible as a method of synthesis. No doubt this is why so many have wanted to see it as the privileged locus of the perennial philosophy. The best interpretation of that phrase, as we have already suggested, is not as denoting a fixed and final body of truths forming a well-rounded whole. There *are* philosophical truths. They have been attained in the past, they are being attained today. But each man must acquire them for himself. Moreover, a truth is such precisely because it is anchored in reality and reality, the things that are, beckons us beyond what we have already attained. In going beyond it would be foolish not to try to profit from what others have had to say and profiting from them is precisely to put them to the test of reality. If Thomism meant only what Aquinas taught, it would mean much but not enough to explain why the Church has placed such hope in the future of Thomism. That future Thomism is in our hands. It is something to be won, something to be devised, something that will never achieve the perfection of a "system." The Church cannot have wanted us to turn our backs on our own times and look with nostalgia toward the thirteenth century. Equally, the Church does not want us to look to the future as if there were no past, as if nothing has been settled or could be settled. To strike the difficult balance between old and new is surely the profoundest sense of renewal, of *aggiornamento*.

Envoi

Let me, with a throat raw from preaching without authority, bring this essay to a close. The question before us was the present status of Thomism. It is raised most often by those who feel that the day of the hegemony of Aquinas is over.

In looking at their reasons, we have found some unsound and others sound. If Thomism were only what it has been, its future would deserve to be no brighter than its past. But when Thomism is considered as what it might be, as the task the Church has set us in giving all that advice, it is difficult to see it in conflict with the legitimate desires of its current opponents. For the Thomism we are all called to help bring forth is not *a* philosophy. Here is the genius and inspiration of the Church, it seems to me, in selecting St. Thomas Aquinas as the model and mentor of the intellectual life of Catholics. Both saint and scholar, Thomas Aquinas is the fitting guide of an introduction to philosophy which introduces to philosophy without qualification, to philosophy in all its scope, in all its appearances and efforts. It is the utter catholicity of Aquinas' interests that earns him the role of patron of the Catholic intellectual. To the degree that we exhibit in our own philosophizing the zest and daring of his spirit, we will be worthy of the title, Thomist.

NOTES

1. S. Ramirez, "The Authority of St. Thomas Aquinas," *The Thomist*, Vol. XV, No. 1 (1952), pp. 1–109.

2. See "Toward a Philosophically Ordered Thomism," "Leo XIII and the Philosophical Approach to Modernity," and "Thomism in College" in *Three Paths in Philosophy*, Chicago, 1962.

3. Decree on Christian Education, Introduction, *New York Times*, October 29, 1965.

4. *Ibid.*

5. Address of Pope Paul VI to Participants in the Sixth International Congress of the Pontifical Academy of Saint Thomas Aquinas, September 10, 1965.

6. Josiah Royce, "Pope Leo's Philosophical Movement and its Relations to Modern Thought," in *Fugitive Essays*, Cambridge, Mass., 1920, p. 408.

7. *Ibid.*, p. 429.

8. *Epist. to Coloss.*, 2:8.

9. James A. Weisheipl, O.P., *Thomism as a Perennial Philosophy*, Chicago, 1956, pp. 13–14.

10. Pius XII, *Humani generis*, n. 30.

11. C. S. Lewis, *Studies in Words*, Cambridge, 1960.

12. *Summa theologiae*, Ia, q. 107, a. 1, ad 2m.

13. *Ia*, q. 107, a. 2.

14. O. Bird, *The New Scholasticism*, XXVII, 2, pp. 129–159.

15. J. Maritain, *The Uses of Philosophy*, Princeton, 1961.